"Doing Your Best Is Not Good Enough. You Have to Know What to Do. Then Do Your Best."

W.E. Deming

—— ∽ ❊ ⌘ ——

To *my wonderful wife for her unwavering support and encouragement.*

To *my children who inspire my hopes and dreams.*

*Special thanks to all my selling companions who labor
on the road less traveled. The road of commissions and quotas,
wins and losses, joys and heartaches, independence and bondage.
In other words, the best damn job in the world!*

Finally, to Forrest for helping me face my dragon.

QUEST*for* Success Selling Series

Series I

Sales Lead to Sales Leader

7STEPS FOR
TAKING CONTROL OF
YOUR SALES DESTINY

Sales Lead to Sales Leadership

Doing Your Best Is Not Good Enough.
You Have to Know What to Do.
Then Do Your Best.

DAVID DANIELSON

 **Turning Point Press**

Contents

Sales Lead ⊙ Sales Leader

Contents

Sales Lead⬤Sales Leadership

Contents

Manager's Corner – Chapter 6

Manager's Corner – Chapter 7

Appendix

Introduction:

Who Should Read This Book?

The Quest for Success Selling Series is written for two groups of individuals. The first half of this book, **Sales Lead to Sales Leader**, is written for sales professionals; those on the front lines of the selling battle field; the individual contributors. The second half, **Sales Lead to Sales Leadership**, is written for sales managers and sales executives; the sales generals and captains who lead the troops into battle (as well as those who direct the troops from the bunkers at headquarters).

For my fellow sales managers and executives, I would expect that you would start with Step 1 and fully read and digest **Sales Lead to Sales Leader** for obvious reasons – you should understand and internalize the methodology as well as your team. For my fellow sales professionals, after you finish reading **Sales Lead to Sales Leader** I would encourage you to also fully read the **Manager's Corner**. The perspective you will gain relative to the trials and tribulations of managing a sales organization should accomplish two things. One, help you gain a better understanding of the challenging world your manager lives in. And two, through that understanding help you work together more effectively to achieve your common objective; selling success.

1

From both perspectives, understanding and cooperation is the ideal environment for sales prosperity.

In my 30 year career in sales, I have both managed and trained sales professionals who worked in market segments ranging from high-tech to industrial; from services to capital equipment; from used car sales to implantable medical devices; and from phone sales to door-to-door sales. The average selling price for a single sales transaction has ranged from less than $100 up to $500,000,000. In fact, when I share with some of my class participants that some of the sales professionals I teach close deals worth hundreds of millions of dollars they always say. "Wow, those guys must be really good." Guess what? The main difference between sales reps closing half a billion dollar deals and those who sell $100 deals is not selling skills at all. 99% of the time the difference is the depth of product and market segment knowledge. In fact, if you were a fly on the wall in one of my so-called 'high-end' training sessions, you would be very surprised at how much parity there is between the half a billion dollar group and the $100 group in terms of selling skills such as qualifying, handling objections, competitive positioning and negotiating.

There's an old saying in sales; 'People buy from people'. It really is true. At the end of all this sales methodology stuff and after all the sales process diagrams, in just about every sales transaction, a flesh and blood individual makes a decision to purchase a product or service from another flesh and blood individual. The link between the half a billion dollar sales rep and the $100 rep is really their humanity, along with all their inherent virtues and flaws: Motivated or unmotivated; friendly or impersonal; aggressive or passive; organized or scattered; empathetic or mercenary; etc, etc. The fact is, while the deal size may change in scale, and while some may ride glass elevators to the top floors of office towers to meet with executives in mahogany paneled board rooms sitting at 20 foot long conference tables, others are literally stepping over sleeping dogs making their way into business owner's back offices to sit in chairs with more stains on them than a front row seat at a Gallagher comedy act. The selling skills I have seen from Boston to Bangalore and Seattle to Shanghai are pretty much the same. In the majority of cases, we're all in the same boat. And, in case you haven't noticed, it's not a cruise ship either. It's a lifeboat! We'll talk more about the lifeboat drill later on in The Burning Platform chapter.

The point is whether you sell a product or a service, step into boardrooms or step over dogs, sell as an individual contributor or manage a legion of sales professionals, the **7 Steps for Taking Control of Your Sales Destiny** applies to *everyone* who sells. Success in selling requires extraordinary commitment. Which brings us to

Step 1 in the **7 Steps for Taking Control of Your Sales Destiny**.

Step 1: Stop making excuses and make a commitment to change.

Step 2: More calls will always result in more sales.

Step 3: Qualified activity will *always* result in higher sales effectiveness.

Step 4: "You don't want to buy my product today, do you?" Not a very unique message is it? A unique message speaks to the customer's need to solve their critical business issues, not your critical need to sell them something.

Step 5: "I think I'll buy from you because I like you, and you gave a great presentation." Not the typical response from most customers. No, instead they say things like "I'm sorry. But despite all of your slick talk, fancy presentations, elaborate ROI's and proposals, we just don't see the value in your offering. But hey, thanks for coming by. Give us a call in 5 years or so." OK, they don't say it like that out loud but that's what they're really thinking. Value is not communicated through slick talk and animated PowerPoint presentations. Value is established by connecting your solution to the customer's need to mitigate their issues and achieve their critical business objectives.

Step 6: Out of the thousands of sales professionals I have trained, not a single one sold in an environment where they had zero competition. The fiercely competitive landscape we sell in has established value as the cost of entry in the game. Superior Value is the bar for winning.

Step 7: The old expression is really true. There is never enough time to do it right, but there is always enough time to do it over. Errors in execution of the selling process, including the first 6 steps of the **7 Steps for Taking Control of Your Sales Destiny**, delivers little value to you, your company or your customer. Flawless execution that takes too much time is equally of little value. Doing it right, with speed and quality is of high value to everyone in the process. This is what we call *Time to Value*. Guess what else? Time to value means more time! Oh, to have one more week, one more day, even a few more hours at the end of the month or quarter to get that last deal in. "I'm sorry. But the quarter is now closed. But hey, thanks for playing. Come back again next quarter. In fact, you better come back again next quarter not only with the deal that just slipped but another deal to make up your year-to-date quota."

Every process begins with raw materials that "feed the beast" designed to produce a finished product at the end of the line. For us in sales, the raw materials are sales leads. The finished product is obviously closed sales. The efficiency of the system is measured by how well the process uses, or exploits the raw materials (sales leads), entering the front of the process (our sales funnel), to produce a quality product (closed sales). Inefficient processes produce waste and poor quality. For us that means lost deals and missed forecasts. So here's the question. How well are you presiding over the process of taking in raw sales leads and turning them into closed deals at the end of the sales process? As you will see from some alarming statistics in The Burning Platform chapter, as a group, "we ain't doing so good" in this effort. When the fruit of our efforts results in lost deals, we clearly are not positioning ourselves as sales leaders. However, when we successfully and consistently navigate sales leads to close, we are recognized as true sales leaders. Showing you how to consistently go from Sales Lead to Sales Leader is why I wrote this book.

Once again, whether you're riding up glass elevators or stepping over dogs all day long, you need the **7 Steps for Taking Control of Your Sales Destiny.**

Who should read this book? That's easy. YOU!

QUEST *for* Success Selling Series

Series I

Sales Lead ⓣⓞ Sales Leader

7STEPS FOR
TAKING CONTROL OF
YOUR SALES DESTINY

Series Overview:

Series I

Stop Whining...
Get Busy...
Get Smart & Sell!

Step 1: **Stop Whining...**
▸ **Are You in Control of Your Sales Destiny?**
▸ **Action Requires Commitment**

Step 2: **Get Busy...**
Sales Activity

Step 3: **Get Smart & Sell!**
Qualified Activity

Selling is without question a tough business. When you're selling (meeting or exceeding quota), life is great! You are respected at your company; you're making lots of money; and, your job is secure. However, when you are not selling, quite frankly, life sucks! Instead of being looked at as an asset to your company, you're seen as a burden. You're not making money so not only are you miserable at work, you can also have huge issues in your personal life. Sadly, studies point to money problems as the number one reason for divorce. Finally, the worst part of not selling is your job is anything but secure. At the time of this writing, I can tell you I get at least one phone call a week from someone I know, or I hear about a friend-of-a-friend, who has lost their job in sales. Having said this, I do not feel guilty at all about painting a brutally honest picture, albeit somewhat discouraging, of the situation that exists today for sales professionals. Why? Because if you are in the sales game, I know I am not telling you a single thing you don't already know.

If you are one of the fortunate who are meeting or exceeding sales quota, congratulations on your accomplishment and congratulations for taking the initiative to read the **7 Steps for Taking Control of Your Sales Destiny.** What you are going to learn in Series I will most certainly help you sustain and surpass your current level of performance. If you are one of those who are doing ok, not exactly hitting it out of the park, and you're trying to figure out how to take your game to the next level, Series I is going to serve as a great spring training session getting you refocused on the fundamentals of what it takes to win in selling. If on the other hand you find yourself struggling to meet sales objectives, **Stop Whining... Get Busy... Get Smart & Sell** is exactly the coaching you need at this moment. Challenging times can create tremendous stress and anxiety. Stress and anxiety can easily lead to paralysis; spending too much time worrying about what to do rather than actually doing what you should do. Paralysis in sales is deadly. Now is not the time to complain about what you *can't do*. Now is the time to focus on what you *can do* and just get busy doing it. In other words, proceed to the introduction and start reading immediately!

Series II

Shut Up & Listen... Say 'So What' & Sell!

Step 4:	**Shut Up & Listen...**
	Unique Message
Step 5:	**Say 'So What' & Sell!**
	Establish Value

OK, you've finished reading Series I, **Stop Whining... Get Busy & Sell**. Which means you have put away your crying towel, pushed the busy work where it belongs – at the back of your priority list, and you're engaging in quality activity. Congratulations! You're now ready for Series II, **Shut Up & Listen... Say 'So What' & Sell**.

Just about every client I have worked with has asked me to deliver training sessions on business development (lead generation, prospecting, pipeline building etc). A few years ago the president of one particular client of mine requested that I put together a training course on how to penetrate large accounts. The challenges they faced were typical. How do we identify who we should be contacting within the target organization? Who are the people with power and influence and how do we reach them? How do we navigate past the gatekeepers? How do we create interest and urgency in the first 20 seconds of a phone call in the event we actually do get to speak to a live breathing prospect?

Of course my response was, "Sure, we can put together a program". However, I did follow up with a simple question for this executive. "Let's say we train the sales team to be more effective at business development within large accounts and they actually do start getting scheduled meetings with individuals who have power and influence in the organization. When they have that audience and are face-to-face up to their eyeballs in the 'moment-of-truth', what the heck are they going to say?" You and I both know what the majority of sales reps say in this situation. "Hi I'm So-and-So from XYZ Company. Thanks for allowing us to meet with you today. So... How's business?" What a fantastic, well prepared, take my breath away, original question! Or, how about this popular approach: "Hi I'm So-and-So from XYZ Company. Thanks for allowing us to meet with you today. We would like to begin this meeting with a short 57 slide PowerPoint presentation introducing you to our company. By the way I have brought along a fully loaded handgun in the event that at any time during this exciting presentation, which is all about how great we are, you may decide to pull the trigger and put yourself out of your misery."

What's that? You actually delivered or participated in a few business development meetings exactly like these two examples just this past week? So that's why a recent survey showed that 3 out of 4 executives feel that sales calls are a complete waste of time. And, here's a question for all of you sales managers. How many meetings exactly like this are going to be conducted this week by your sales team? It's a frightening number to contemplate isn't it?

Series II is about learning how to do two things. First, how to shut up instead of wasting the customer's time by talking their ears off about things they have little interest in. Second, how to identify tangible value from the customer's perspective, not yours. When you do these two things your message becomes truly unique. Rather than a message of, "Hey, my company, my product and I are so fantastic, you would be absolutely crazy not to want to do business with us. By the way, now that I have taken up all of our time talking about us, I'm afraid we don't have any time to talk about you. So…you don't want to buy something today, do you?" Or, how about this one? "Hey, I really was too busy to do any research on your company and your industry before this meeting. So, in terms of being prepared with a set of highly relevant questions focused on the specific critical business challenges you are facing and how those challenges are impacting your ability to achieve your current business objectives, why don't I just ask you; How's business?"

Of course, no one reading this book says these exact words at all. Right? Well, it's probably not exactly what you say, but trust me; for your customer it is exactly what they are hearing. By the way, how's that working out for you? Another recent voice of the customer survey indicated that 82% of sales reps are unprepared for meetings. Does that statistic surprise you at all?

In Series II you will also learn about the two most powerful words in selling; **So What!** Customer says, "Hello." You say, "**So what** is your current situation?" Customer says, "I've got problems." You say, "**So what** is causing these problems?" Customer says, "X, Y and Z are causing these problems." You say, "**So what** other problems are being created and what are the causes behind those?" Customer says, "These are the additional problems and here's what's causing them." You say, "**So what** is the impact of all of these problems on the company, your team, and you?" Customer says, "It ain't good…especially for me personally" You say, "**So what** kind of number would you put on ain't good?" Customer says, "X number of dollars, time, lost productivity, aggravation, etc." You say, "**So what** is going to happen if these problems which are having X impact on the company, the team and you, are not resolved in the next 3, 6 or 12 months?" Customer says, "Uh-oh! I better do something fast to resolve these issues." You say, "**So what** would you say your level of urgency is for a solution on a scale of 1 to 10?" Customer says, "10!" You say, "**So what** are you going to do about it?" Customer says, "Uh…could you help me?" Voila! The power of **So What!**

So What! are indeed the two most powerful words in selling. Most importantly, whoever is saying **So What** is in control of the conversation. Let me say that again. Whoever is saying **So What** is in control of the conversation. It's like having the serve in tennis. The person saying **So What** is on the offensive. The person answering **So What** is on the defensive. Typically, we sales folks are not so good at serving. In fact, our serve stinks. Example: Customer says, "Hello." Meaning, "OK, I'm ready to take your serve. Give it to me." We then serve up a 50 mph marshmallow like, "Thanks for having us in today. What we would like to do is start our meeting with a brief presentation about our company." Customer says, "OK." In reality, the customer is thinking, "**So What!** I've heard this spiel a bazillion times before. Why don't you just shoot me now and get it over with." Some customers will exhibit the tolerance to sit and wait until you're done. Others will stop you after about 5 minutes and say, "**So what** does all this mean to me and my business? And by the way; **So what** does it cost?" The customer has taken over the serve and is now on the offensive and in control. Sound familiar? Ready for Series II? It really is time to **Shut Up & Listen... Say 'So What' & Sell**.

Get Mean...
Get LEAN & Sell!

Step 6:   **Get Mean...**
          Superior Value

Step 7:   **Get Lean & Sell!**
          Time to Value

Even when we execute steps 1 through 5 with great proficiency, the customer is very likely to say, **So What!** Meaning, the customer still perceives your offering and your company as only equal or perhaps inferior to a competitive alternative. If you are perceived as the same or inferior you are certainly not different than the alternative. If you're not different you are not relevant in the eyes of the customer. If you are not relevant your offering has diminished value or perhaps no value at all. Not a desirable position to be in if you are looking to win. This is where Step 6 and Superior Value come into play.

Customers demand value. Distilled down to the simplest equation, whoever provides superior value wins. However, here's where it gets confusion to us on the selling side. The customer's perception of value may not match our perception of value. We think we have the best product or service. The customer thinks our competitor does. We think the competition sucks. The customer thinks they're great and we suck. Who's right? This part is simple. Whoever signs the order and the check is right. If the customer, for whatever irrational reason, thinks we suck, then we suck! It's our job to change the customer's perception and ultimately convince them otherwise. Here are some Superior Value ground rules you'll learn about in Series III.

1. There is always a competitor. It may be an alternative resource, it may be internal budget dollars, or it may be inactivity you are competing against. In any case, there is always a competitor.

2. When it comes to competitive positioning, how we stack up against the competition, the customer is always right. Perception is reality. This is their truth and our starting point.

3. Only the customer can define value. No matter how convicted we may be, we cannot define it for them.

4. Our job is to influence the customer's thinking to convince them that we indeed provide Superior Value to all competitive alternatives.

5. It is impossible to position your product or service until you know where you stand in the mind of the customer. This means you must understand the customer's view of the strengths and weakness of your offering vs. your competitor's.

It really is as simple as the famous quote by Ruth Stafford Peale (wife of *The Power of Positive Thinking* author Norman Vincent Peale), *"Find a need and fill it."*

As sales professionals, our job is to:

• Find or discover the customer's need. Is it compelling enough for the customer to take action and buy something?

• Quantify it. Determine how big it is.

• Qualify our competitive positioning. Determine where we stand in the customer's mind.

- Fill the need in a way that delivers Superior Value to the customer.

- Get mean and pursue all the above activities pro-actively!

When it comes to establishing Superior Value in the face of fierce competitive forces, it is absolutely critical that we be pro-active vs. passive in our approach. This is the time to get mean! The sooner we face our enemy, the sooner we can begin to competitively position our solution. Those who wait, or passively choose not to engage the enemy, are simply failing to take control of their sales destiny and are instead placing their fate in the hands of their customers. Sadly, in many cases they forfeit the battle by simply failing to engage.

Success in business requires that we do two things really well. First, whatever it is we do, we do it right. Second, we do it with speed. The same is true in selling. Executing the sales process 'right' is only half of the formula for success. Because we sell in highly competitive environments we must not only execute the sales process to the highest degree of performance standards, we must also execute with speed. Doing it right puts us on the playing field in terms of delivering value to our customers. Doing it with speed empowers us to outflank our competition. Ultimately, in the eyes of our customers, doing it right with speed defines quality. Again, customers demand value, and they want it delivered with speed and wrapped up in a pretty bow of quality. *Time to value* is the operative phrase.

When you first call on a customer, rather than spending their time listening to you talk about yourself, they want you to invest time talking about how you are going to help them solve their critical business issues. That's time to value! Going unprepared to a meeting without all of the information or materials you may need, "Oh, I'm sorry, I left that information at the office. When I get back I'll e-mail it to you..." is not time to value. Errors in your presentation or proposals is not professional, not quality, and not time to value for your customers. "I'll have the answers to your questions right away." Sounds good. However, calling the customer back a week later is not time to value. Calling a lead from a trade show 6 months after the event is not time to value. I remember one particular incident of this at a Fortune 10 company I once worked for. Our business development team was making follow up phone calls to the lead data base from our last trade show. Unfortunately, it took us 6 months to contact some of these leads. At that point, a number of the responses were; "Oh, thanks for calling. I actually bought a system from your competitor 3 months ago. You guys just never followed up with me."

In Series III you will learn about the power of doing it right, doing it with speed, and doing it with quality in everything. That's *Time to Value!*

The Burning Platform:

The Experts Say Our Sales Productivity **Stinks!** Are They Right?

"Oh really!" you may be saying to yourself. "So where does this guy get off trashing our sales productivity? And by the way, what horse did he come in on anyway?" Well, let me start by validating the horse that I rode in on. I have 30 years of sales and sales management experience, which includes 15 years of delivering sales training to some of the premier global companies in the world. "So What?" So, I've been where you are right now and here's why I know from experience that our sales productivity stinks. As part of the system, I have been one of the biggest offenders! That's right. There have been times in my career when I stunk it up pretty good. In fact, until I learned differently, I was a huge part of the problem. Secondly, when I say that our sales productivity stinks, it's not just my opinion, it is a quantifiable fact based on the CSO

Insights 2009 Survey Results and Analysis on Sales Performance Optimization.

Let's stop for a few moments for a deeper dive into some of the CSO numbers. Imagine you are a participant in one of my sales training classes. I'm going to write some numbers on the flip charts on the following pages. See if you can tell me what the numbers mean. (Hint: The answers are to the right of each flip chart.) After each set of numbers I'm going to ask you a question. Feel free to write your answers in the book.

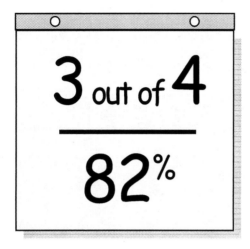

3 out of 4 senior executives feel sales calls are a waste of time.
Simon Bradstock, Vice President, Corporate Products, Dow Jones

82% of sales reps are unprepared for meetings.
Sirius Decisions, Inc.

According to the American Marketing Association, 50% to 80% of marketing content goes unused by sales reps.

How effective are you at conducting 'Time-to-Value' sales meetings with your customers?

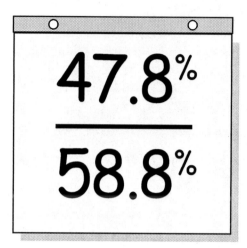

47.8% / 58.8%

Only 47.8% of forecasted deals are won.

Just 58.8% of sales reps are meeting or exceeding quota expectations. This number is down from a peak of 61% in 2008.

CSO Insights 2009 Sales Performance Optimization Report

40% 29% / 1 in 4

40% of reps barely bother with their company's sales process. Another 29% use it just over half the time.

1 in 4 reps use it infrequently or irregularly, even though consistency correlates with significantly better overall sales performance.

CSO Insights 2008 Sales Performance Optimization Report

What is your forecast accuracy & where are you in terms of meeting quota expectations?

How would you rate your execution of your company's established sales process?

Forrester® reports that for companies surveyed, just over 50% rate their execution of Best Practices in selling as 'poor to average'.

CSO Insights reports that 49.7% of companies surveyed rate Best Practice sharing as 'needs improvement'.

Given your company's investment in sales training, how would you rate your execution and sharing of best practices?

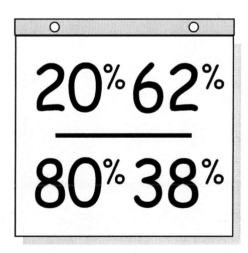

2009 CSO Insights: 20% of sales reps are generating 62% of sales revenue.

The remaining 80% of the sales team generate only 38% of revenue.

Part of the 'Vital Few' or the 'Trivial Many': Where do you fall in the 80/20 Rule?

According to Microsoft Business Solutions, 44% of sales directors admit that fewer than 80% of their staff are using CRM technology effectively.

Sales directors themselves are hardly blameless with 72% confessing that they tolerate inefficient use of the CRM they have invested in.

A mighty 73% do not discipline staff who fail to use CRM systems.

Microsoft Business Solutions

Part of the solution or part of the problem:

How would you rate your management team's ability to leverage the investment your company has made in your CRM implementation?

I think it's always good to provide perspective prior to making a compelling argument. In fact, if the numbers we just reviewed are not in themselves compelling to you, if these numbers do not make at least some of the hairs on the back of your neck stand up, you are either working for a company that is completely anomalous to the 1,500 companies surveyed by CSO Insights, or you are working a sales territory located in the state of denial!

The sense of urgency I am trying to create is called a burning platform. Take a look around you my friend. That heat you're feeling is not from sitting too close to the barbecue on your deck while sipping on a cold libation. The heat is coming from the most challenging selling environment we have ever experienced in our selling careers; in my case 30 years. Remember the lifeboat drill? Guess what? THIS IS NOT A DRILL! It's real! Sales professionals who are not performing are being terminated. It's very likely you have at least one colleague who has experienced this terrible fate. The question is what about you? What are you going to do to improve your own performance so you get to stay in the boat?

I wrote the **7 Steps for Taking Control of Your Sales Destiny** for one reason. I want to provide you, my fellow sales professionals who are unconditionally committed to success — ready willing and able to do everything it takes to win including all the hard work, and unwilling to accept failure as an option, a practical tool for taking control of your sales destiny. If you are one of those individuals who share my love, affection and unyielding commitment to the profession of selling, you and I are going to share an exciting journey together. So let's get started!

Step 1:

Stop Whining...

Are You in Control of Your Sales Destiny?

If you are not meeting your professional and personal sales goals, the fact is: **You are not in control of your sales destiny!**

"Now wait a minute! I've got mitigating circumstances. Surely there are a few exceptions." OK, there are two I can think of. If you have been selling for less than one year, you are probably still learning how to sell, still learning your product and your market, and still building a pipeline of qualified prospects. If this is your situation you get a pass for the moment. The second exception is for those who find themselves in a particular industry profoundly impacted by an economic downturn. For example, at the time of this writing, the mortgage, real estate and related industries. That is not to say that there aren't individuals in these industries who are, in spite of the downturn, successfully selling. However, it is safe to say that many have been negatively impacted by recent economic forces outside of their control. You too get a pass, for now, if this describes your situation.

However, these two exceptions do not dismiss the rest of us who currently sell in increasingly challenged markets due to decreased demand, budget and spending cutbacks, and ever present and growing competitive pressures. For us there is no escape from or excuse for poor sales performance. The cold hard fact we must face as sales professionals is this:

**Poor Sales Performance is Not About
Your Company, Your Manager, Your Product,
Your Marketing Campaign,
Your Customers, the Market Conditions,
or Even Your Competition.**

It's About You!

"Now hold on a minute, Dave…" Yes, I know what you are going to say next. After 30 years of selling, I know what you are going to say because I've said it all myself; in fact, numerous times over the years. "My company doesn't even have a sales process." "The process we have is 14 steps long with 27 sub-steps." "By the way, our CRM system is nothing but a burden and a waste of my valuable time." "My manager cares about one thing and one thing only – numbers! They don't manage me like I'm a flesh and blood sales professional, they manage me like I'm some kind of sales machine expected to churn out orders like a chicken laying eggs. By the way, have you ever asked a chicken what it feels like to pass an egg?" "Marketing? You're kidding, right? What marketing!" "Hey, customers are just not buying right now. The market is really tough." "There is no such thing as customer loyalty anymore. Customers just go for the best price." "The competition is getting tougher and tougher. They make deals my company is not willing to make. As a result, I lose the sale." "Oh, one more thing. In some ways, the competition really is better than we are. That makes it really tough to defend against. Maybe I should be working for them."

Guess what? All of these things are true to a degree in some cases, and in other cases perhaps true to the nth degree. So why then do I say that poor sales performance is not about your company, your manager, your product, your customer, the market or your competition? Because despite how true all of these things may be, the fact is, there is virtually nothing you can do to change any of these dynamics. Take it from someone who has tried and failed many times. As a sales rep on the front lines every day, your chances of changing your company, your manager, the marketing programs, etc., are about as good as a snowball's chances in a pizza oven on Super Bowl Sunday.

Case in point: I was working for a company in 2004 as a Regional Sales Director. By that time in my career, I had been selling and managing for 24 years; I had founded and operated a very successful marketing and promotions company in Atlanta from 1982 to 1990. And, I had also traveled the world conducting sales training classes in the mid-90's. In other words, I had a pretty good level of experience relating to sales, sales training and marketing. Not unlike many companies, the company I was working for had their share of problems and challenges both internally and in the market place. Naturally, I thought I had some good ideas that might help us improve our marketing effectiveness and sales performance. So what did I do? I wrote numerous lengthy emails to my boss sharing my ideas for change. Guess what happened? It went something like this; "Dave, thanks for the input. You have some good ideas here. Let's discuss in more detail when we can schedule some time together." Guess when that time came? The day I left the company, I was still waiting. However, there is a happy ending to this story. When I did finally leave to go back to sales consulting and training, this very company became one of my best customers. In my new role as consultant and provider of sales training how do you think my ideas were received? "Dave, I agree 100% with the sales training program you have proposed. When can we get started?" In fact, my endorsement did not stop with my executive sponsor, the VP of Sales; it went all the way to the CEO and the Chairman of the Board who dialogued with me regularly regarding the program. The cold reality and the moral of the story is this; when you are one of the rank and file, it is almost impossible to get the generals to listen to you and adopt your ideas for change.

I am reminded of something a customer of mine told me back in the mid 80's. John owned an incentive and premium business with a focus on sales incentive programs. Obviously, John's business depended on his clients nurturing, recognizing and rewarding the individuals in their sales organizations. Something most companies are, all too often, too busy to do. John's sales mission was to get his customers to recognize the untapped value and contribution the sales team could bring to the business. In his sales pitch he would say the following; "The best consultant you could ever hire is already on your payroll. The problem is you just aren't listening or motivating them to help you solve your problems." Despite their best efforts to change, within most corporations little has improved from the time John relayed this statement to me. Sadly, the culture in most companies simply does not facilitate input from the rank and file.

Here's one more valuable lesson I learned from my national sales manager at my first sales job in 1980. Shortly after I started in my role as the regional sales executive for the southeast, Kurt told me he was being reassigned within the organization. I could see from Kurt's obvious frustration that he clearly did not agree with the move. In fact, he gave me the impression that he was just another pawn on the corporate chessboard being pushed around by the powers that be, completely at their will and not his own. When I asked him the reason for the sudden move he summed up the rationale as follows; "Dave, the game doesn't change. Only the players do." In my experience I have found Kurt's assessment pretty much spot on.

I'm sure you have a hundred examples similar to my few experiences. Does the reality of the situation mean we all actually don't deserve to have better bosses? Does it mean that our companies couldn't treat us with a little more respect and attentiveness? Hey, would it kill marketing to come up with just one or two truly effective campaigns that would provide us with a just few more qualified leads? Would our customers go out of business if they exhibited a little more loyalty towards us for Pete's sake? Would it put us out of business if we at least looked at some programs that would level the playing field with our competitors? Of course not! I understand this, and certainly we could benefit from positive change in all of these areas. However, I also understand that as much as these changes may be need-ed, as right as you may be in recommending them, the fact remains that it is nearly impossible to change the game unless you are one of the folks making the rules. As my first district sales manager told me years ago; "Dave, stop thinking about what we could be or should be doing. We've got to sell what we have in our bag today!" Not only do we have to sell what we have today; we have to sell in the environment that exists today whatever that may be in regard to company, manage-ment, product, market, customers or competition. That is the current playing field we are on, and we have little power to change the game.

If you can't change the game, what can you change? There truly is only one thing you have complete power to change. You! Time for our first of many **Quest** *for* **Success Directives**.

Quest *for* **Success Directive #1:**
The road to sales success is about you and nothing else because nothing else is truly in your control!

Stop Trying to Change Things That Are Not In Your Control!

In fact, to place your hopes for success in the things you cannot change is an exercise in speculation, frustra-tion and futility.

Waiting is Not a Strategy!

Still holding out for an alternative strategy? OK then, if not change, what about the 'lay siege' strategy? What if we just surround the fortress, pitch our tents and wait it out? Let me ask you something. How many times have you waited for change in your career? A change such as a better process or manager, a new and improved product release, a new marketing campaign that rains down qualified leads from the heavens, a turn around in the market, a change of heart in customers who now value loyalty over price, or how about some kinder and gentler competitors? Hey, be patient! Things can only get better; right? Let's just sit here in our tents and wait for a change.

Okay, so we waited, and guess what happened? The new process is different, but it's still inefficient! The new manager was great for the first 30 days. But now they seem to be just like the old manager; numbers, numbers, numbers. Hey, did you see the new marketing campaign? Looks great, but where are the leads? Looks like the market is going to stay flat for another quarter. I don't think my customers got the memo on how we all agreed to focus on value instead of price. I ran into my competition at the bid opening yesterday. You know what she said to me? "Hey, I've got more than enough business from your customers on my plate already. Why don't you take this one?" Sure, laying siege is a great strategy. Let's just wait it out because 'a change is a coming'. Sounds more like a campaign slogan than a realistic strategy.

In my experience a large number of those who waited for change are still waiting, while the rest waited themselves out of a job, and, in some cases, a profession.

> **Quest *for* Success Directive #2:**
> Waiting is not a strategy!
> ## Stop Waiting for Change!

The Blame Game – An Excuse for Failure

There is a third strategy which I have found all too prevalent among sales teams. The 'it's not me, it's them, so I'll blame everything else strategy'. This strategy is usually adopted out of frustration after the waiting for change approach has failed. "Hey, it's not my fault I'm not selling. Our product stinks!" "I'm not getting any leads." "My manager doesn't know how to manage." "My company doesn't care." "Buyers are liars, and the competition is unfair." Sound familiar? Oh not from any of you reading this book, but we've heard others complain; right?

I remember one national sales meeting in Chicago hosted by our world-wide managing director. One of the regional sales managers was trying to rationalize his team's poor sales performance in the previous quarter. "We were faced with unfair competition particularly on the part of XYZ company..." As he continued, the managing director quickly interrupted, "Excuse me; there is no such thing as unfair competition. There is only competition." "Yes," the manager continued, "but what they were doing was placing systems on trial with customers, which is something we do not do, so..." "Excuse me," the managing director interjected again, "There is no such thing as unfair competition." The discussion ping-ponged back and forth for a few more minutes before the manager finally understood the point. What our managing director was saying is we cannot control what the competition does. What they do or don't do is not a matter of being fair or unfair. It is simply what we must deal with in a competitive marketplace. Essentially, all is fair in love, war and sales. To blame the competition for our poor sales performance, and accuse them of not being fair, is in reality shirking our own responsibility and accountability. Finally the manager understood and was forced to focus on the real reasons for his team's poor sales performance. Specifically, poor call activity, poor qualifying, poor prospecting, poor execution of the step-of-sale process, poor differentiation regarding the competitive offering, etc., etc. It is always so much easier to point the finger at someone else; in this case, the competition and the company's policy of no trial systems. However, our managing director was having none of it and forced not only this manager, but all of us in the room to realize that poor sales performance results cannot be hung around the necks of others or mitigated by the current circumstances. We are the ones to be held accountable.

On the other hand, over the years, I have had the privilege of working with, managing and training what I call true sales pros; the elite sales reps, the heavy hitters, the players and the horses. These are the perennial President's Club Winners making the trips to the Caribbean, Cancun, Tahiti and other exotic places around the globe. While I can't elaborate here exactly what each one of those sales pros did to succeed, I can tell you with 100% accuracy what they did not do. None of them tried to change things that were out of their control. None of them waited for change. And, none of them blamed others, or the circumstances, for their failures. Instead, all of them recognized and understood the things that were not in their control to change. Therefore, they chose to change what was in their control; themselves. To them, the product, the company, management, the market, the customer and the competition were simply the rules of the game and the lines marking the playing field. For example, when a basketball player steps on the out of bounds line with the ball, gets whistled by the official and then must turn the ball over to the other team, you don't see them jump up and down and curse at the painted line on the court. What you do see them do is hand the ball to the official, turn to their team members while pointing at themselves and say, "My bad." Meaning, "Sorry guys. That was my mistake and my fault." True professionals don't blame the rules, the officials or the playing field. They don't get out their crying towels, make excuses and blame everything, and everyone else, for their failures. When they do (remember John McEnroe's infamous "You can *not* be serious!' tantrum at the 1981 Wimbledon championships), their behavior is viewed as clearly unprofessional. True professionals hold themselves accountable for their mistakes, and then they change their play to improve their chances for success.

By the way, I have seen this quality not only in top sales professionals, but also in many other examples of individual success. Change is not something successful people wait on. Rather than wait for change, successful people choose to make change happen by changing themselves. Notice the word *choose*. It's true; successful people *choose* to succeed, while those who fail *choose* not to succeed by attempting to change what they cannot control, waiting for change, or choosing to blame everything else for their failures.

My personal trainer trains professional athletes in the off-season, and occasionally I have had an opportunity to jump in with them. This past summer I was training with Jamal Lewis, premier running back for the Cleveland Browns. When it comes to choosing to succeed or choosing to fail Jamal summed up the entire subject very plainly when he told me, "We have a saying in the NFL. Coach doesn't cut you. You cut yourself."

Quest *for* **Success Directive #3:**
Playing the blame game is just an excuse for failure.
Stop Blaming Everything & Everyone Else!

So let me ask you a few questions. Are you in control of your sales success? Are you meeting your professional and personal sales goals? If not, what are you doing about it? How do you plan to succeed? Which strategy have you chosen up until now? More importantly, which strategy will you choose from this point on? Are you ready to accept personal responsibility and hold yourself accountable for results? Are you still waiting for change? Or, are you committed to changing the only thing in your control to change? *Yourself!*

Are You Ready to Take Control of Your Sales Destiny?

Here are the first of many Rules of the Road signs you'll be seeing on the journey we will be taking together as you take control of your sales destiny. Which signs will you choose to follow?

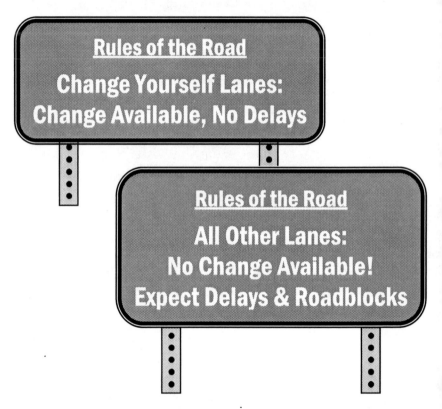

Rules of the Road
Change Yourself Lanes:
Change Available, No Delays

Rules of the Road
All Other Lanes:
No Change Available!
Expect Delays & Roadblocks

Quest *for* **Success Directive #4:**
Are you in control of your sales destiny?
Start Taking Control of Your Sales Destiny
By Changing What You Can - Yourself!

Action Requires Commitment

Taking control of your sales destiny is going to require that you are committed to: Accepting responsibility for your sales performance and holding yourself accountable for your failures. Change what you can – *Yourself!*

In this and subsequent **Quest** *for* **Success Selling Series** books, I will outline how you can take control of your sales destiny in a 7-step process. If you have truly made the above commitments, even without the 7-steps, you have already greatly increased your chances for selling success. Obviously, it is my conviction that armed with the **7 Steps for Taking Control of Your Sales Destiny** you will maximize your potential to reach, surpass and sustain the success you have planned for and desire. However, if you don't share my conviction and you find you are not ready to make the commitment, now would be a good time to close this book and do one of two things; pass it on to a friend or, toss it right in the garbage can! That's right. And by the way, if you choose the garbage can you won't be hurting my feelings. I've already invested the time necessary to write this book, so I'm good. The question is: Why waste your time?

Quest *for* **Success Directive #5:**
Put away your crying towel,

Stop Whining & Sell!

If you've decided to keep on reading, congratulations for taking the initiative to seize control of your sales destiny! Let's get started with these 5 **Quest** *for* **Success Directives.**

Quest *for* **Success Directives**

#1 *Stop trying to change things that are not in your control!*

#2 *Stop waiting for change!*

#3 *Stop blaming everything and everyone else!*

#4 *Start taking control of your sales destiny by changing what you can – Yourself!*

#5 *Put away your crying towel, Stop Whining & Sell!*

Step 2:

Get Busy...

Sales Activity
Busy Work or Busy Working?

When I facilitate this topic in one of my training sessions, I ask the following question: "What do you need to be more successful?" Without question the #1 response is "More leads!" The #2 response is "More qualified leads!" Sound familiar? Here is a list of the typical answers I get.

- More leads
- More qualified leads
- More territory
- Easier financing terms
- Less time spent on administrative tasks (CRM)
- Less time handling customer service issues
- Broader product offering
- More sales support
- Better marketing materials

If we had all of these things, who wouldn't make President's Club every year? Here's my next question to the group. "If you don't get any of these things on your wish list, what is the one thing you can do to get more sales and be more successful?" Usually there is a 15 second or so silence and then someone raises their hand and says, "Make more sales calls." *Yahtzee!*

Now here comes the burning-platform question: "If we are committed to not trying to change things that are not in our control; if we have stopped waiting for change; if we have put away our crying towels and stopped blaming everything and everyone else for our failures; if we are taking control of our sales success by changing what we can — ourselves; why is it no one mentioned making more sales calls when I asked you what you needed to be successful?" This is the part when the frowns of conviction set in on the faces of the participants. Soon after there are a few nods of affirmation. "Can I get an amen from the group?" More nodding. "Who wants to get rescued from this burning-platform?" Finally, hand raises from every participant.

There is no question that selling as an individual contributor (you don't manage a team) is tough. In my view, it's the second hardest job there is in any sales organization (the first is sales manager of a team of individual contributors). Trust me, the pressure on managers to meet sales targets along with the challenge of managing a significant number of reps who are contributing to the CSO statistics, is enough to make your head explode. That's why your managers act the way they do most of the time; as if they are one step ahead of a fit and ready to be committed to an institution. Yes, selling is tough. However, the reality is we make it tougher on ourselves when we focus on the tougher things rather than the easier things.

So what are the easy things to focus on? When it comes to getting more sales, the **7 Steps for Taking Control of Your Sales Destiny** begins with the easiest thing to do: **Sales** Activity. Getting more leads is hard; getting more qualified leads is even harder; getting more territory is hard; getting easier financing terms for your deals is even harder. We could go on and on with the list of the hard things we have to do. However, Step 2, making more calls is easy. You simply go out and make more calls! But wait a minute Dave; there are other things that stand in the way of just making more calls. Oh, you mean things like you need more product-training to feel more comfortable talking about performance and specs, so...can't really talk to the project level folks just yet. Or, your not the best when it comes to financial acumen so...can't make a call on the CFO anytime soon. How about this one? You don't really have a good business development pitch for making cold calls, either on the phone or in person, so...let's not get too aggressive prospecting. I've even heard this one a couple of times. I left the office without any business cards so…can't make a cold call on a new prospect even though they're right next door to the scheduled appointment I just had with an existing customer. You know what I think of every one of these excuses? Bull-hockey! Let me pull the excuse mat right from under your feet and give you another **Quest** *for* **Success** directive.

Quest *for* **Success Directive #6:**
Making sales calls is your #1 objective. All other activities are subordinate to this categorical imperative.

Make More Sales Calls!

How important is this? Well, here's the difference between a hypothetical imperative and a categorical imperative. A hypothetical imperative compels action in a given circumstance. For example, if all the lights are green and all the conditions are favorable, I can make some more sales calls. A categorical imperative, on the other hand, denotes an absolute, unconditional requirement that asserts its authority in *ALL* circumstances. Despite all the roadblocks, regardless of all the things I need to be successful that I don't yet have, whether the lights are green, red, yellow or polka-dotted, I'm still going to make more sales calls. In other words, no waiting for change; no blaming others; no stopping on the side of the road to pull out my crying towel; I'm going to make more calls. That's my categorical imperative. Why? Time for another Rules of the Road sign.

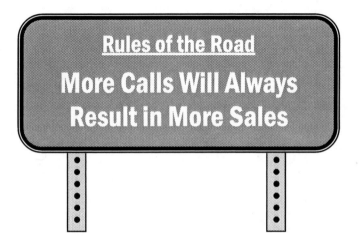

Rules of the Road

More Calls Will Always Result in More Sales

But Dave, you said it's easy to make more calls, but it's not that easy when all these other things I have to deal with get in the way. Alright, you're still not getting the categorical imperative part, but that's okay; it's going to take a little time to break some of your long standing habits and thinking. In fact, it's going to take you exactly 7 days to change, because that's how much time I'm giving you for your next step in the **7 Steps for Taking Control of Your Sales Destiny**. So let's talk about how you make more calls.

The First Thing You've Got To Do Is Take The Stairs!

Back in 1980, one of the first books I read on selling was Zig Ziglar's *See You At The Top*. If you have not read Zig's classic, I would recommend you invest in the latest 25th Anniversary edition. Just go to Amazon and order it. One of the best stories Zig tells in *See You At The Top*, is about his visit with his family to the Washington Monument. At ground level there is an elevator that will take you to the top of the monument. Often times there is a long line of sightseers and therefore a long wait for the elevator. However, as Zig tells it, there is a small sign posted on the wall next to the stairs which says the following: *"There is no waiting to get to the top, if you're willing to take the stairs."* The moral to Zig's story indicts us all. How many of us are standing in a crowded line waiting for the elevator to get to the top of our sales careers. Waiting for more leads, more qualified leads, more territory, a better product, a better boss, etc., etc. When in reality, what we should be doing, is simply taking the initiative to take the stairs of hard work and no excuses.

Quest *for* Success Directive #7:
Stop waiting in line for the elevator to success.
Be Willing to Take the Stairs!

"We Don't Plan to Fail, We Fail to Plan!"

Now this expression has been around even longer than Zig Ziglar. In fact, it was Thomas Paine, author of Common Sense in 1776, who first said it. Like Zig, it may be old school, but it is as accurate today as the day it was first uttered. Here's an example I heard just a short while ago.

A dear friend of mine is a regional sales director with one of my current clients. Ray and I have previously worked together at three companies, including the current company he is with. Ray had been reviewing the previous quarter's results which had fallen short of projections. "I was looking for what went wrong", Ray told me, "and I discovered it was our call activity. I then started calling my team and asked them for their call schedules for the upcoming week. Dave, you would not believe it. Their scheduling is pitiful! Most of them have 3 or 4 meetings on their calendar and the rest is just 'see what happens'. It's incredible!" I had one question for Ray. "Are you actually surprised?" My only surprise was that Ray found the whole situation incredible at all. The fact is, it is sadly all too common.

The performance standard for Ray's team was a minimum of 12 face-to-face calls per week. In reality, they were scheduling an average of 4. As a result, their call activity was nowhere near performance standards. As a result, they did not meet their quota or their forecast. In other words, they did not plan to fail, they failed to plan. Some would argue that what they really did is plan for failure, and I would not disagree with that analysis.

Some years ago I was in Sydney, Australia visiting one of my customers. At the time I was a worldwide channel sales manager, and my customer was an office equipment dealer. I was supporting them in a 3-day open-house event. As part of my trip, I was also going to do some training with their sales team. Sean, the sales manager who was hosting me, was a thirty-something go-getter with a track record of success with the company. Prior to the training, he called me in his office to discuss a problem he was having with one particular salesman. "Dave, I am hoping you can help me with of my sales reps. Doug is a good guy with decent sales skills. However, he has one drastic shortcoming which is standing in the way of his success. He is terrible at planning. He basically flies by the seat of his pants and just takes things as they come rather than scheduling his activity. I really can't understand how someone can work that way to be honest with you. Take me for example. I schedule everything. Today is August 12th. You can ask me what I am doing on Tuesday morning the second week of October and I can tell you. See, its right here in my planner! Please, if you can help me get Doug to start scheduling things, I would really appreciate it." The lesson of this story is not how much I was able to change Doug's scheduling habits in one training session, which as you can imagine was not significantly, but rather the success Sean had achieved from a career of planning and organization.

Unfortunately, organizational skills are not the strong suit of most sales professionals. If it were, we would not be facing the dismal rate of only 48% forecast accuracy, and the percentage of sales reps meeting or exceeding quota would be more than 58.8%. However, fixing the problem is going to require more than simply asking the Doug's of the world to change their unorganized ways and start scheduling all of their activities. "Sure, I can schedule all of my activities. Not a problem! Why didn't you just say so in the first place?" Or how about my friend Ray's team? "Hey Ray, scheduling 12 to 15 face-to-face calls a week ahead of time is not an issue. All you had to do was say so." I'm pressing my big red Office Depot **EASY** button right now. "That was easy!" *NOT!*

I'm not naive enough to think that reading this book will have any more effect on you. Sure, you may be a bit more convicted, but you're not going to change just because I ask you to. So here's what we are going to do. Unless you discover for yourselves how destructive lack of planning is to your success, you simply will not change. You guessed it; time to throw you back on the burning platform.

What I am not going to ask you to do is take thirty minutes on this Friday afternoon to schedule all your activities for next week. Why? Because at least 80% of you won't do it, that's why. What I am going to ask you to do is get a small note pad, or use your PDA or your Outlook on your laptop or desktop, and starting tomorrow record everything you do during the day. That means phone calls, appointments, admin stuff, lunch, down-time, windshield time, etc. Again, record everything you do during the day. Then, next to each entry indicate if that activity is a selling activity, either on the phone or face-to-face, or a non-selling activity. By the way, on the phone or face-to-face solving problems is not a customer selling activity. Stuffing envelops with sales materials you are going to send out to prospects is also not a customer selling activity. Customer selling is time spent face-to-face, or on the phone, qualifying a prospect or talking to a customer engaged in the sales process.

Do this for five consecutive business days. At the end of five business days add up the time you have invested in selling vs. non-selling activities. Also, if you work for a company with established performance standards for call activity, compare your actual call activity against your company's standard. That means you don't count customer service calls as sales calls. Obviously, if you cannot commit to this five day exercise you will be opting out of the **7 Steps for Taking Control of Your Sales Destiny** program.

For the rest of you committed souls, be sure to record *EVERY ACTIVITY* faithfully, and I'll see you back here in five days time. Meaning, stop reading now, and get to work!

Welcome Back!

You may think it's impossible to be OCD (obsessive compulsive disorder) and disorganized at the same time. I assure you as one who has OCD tendencies that it *is* possible. I have struggled with organization throughout my life. However, an exercise like the one you have just completed is exactly the kind of assignment that appeals to my OCD leanings. Not that OCD applies to any of you readers; this is just a personal side bar. Let's get back to you.

How did you do? If you are at all typical, which by definition most of us are, when you added up all of your bona fide customer selling time in comparison to your non-selling time, you are now in a state of mild to extreme shock. Some of you are realizing that you are investing somewhere in the neighborhood of just 30% of your time in true selling activities. Some may be as high as 50%, or even higher in a few cases. On the following page I've put together ten burning platform questions for you. Please take a few minutes to write your answers in the space provided.

1. What % of your time are you *taking* engaging in non-selling activities?

2. What % of your time are you *investing* in selling activities?

3. Why? What is causing this situation?

4. How is this situation impacting your sales performance?

5. How is this situation impacting your company?

6. How is this situation impacting you personally?

7. What will be the impact on your company and you personally if this situation continues for the next 6 to 12 months?

8. What would be the benefits to you of meeting call activity standards?

9. What is the solution?

10. What do you plan to do about it?

If you did not answer question 9 with: I'm going to stop engaging in non-selling activities and start focusing on scheduling customer selling activities, then you my friend do not have an 'explicit need', a profound sense of urgency, to succeed in sales. We'll get to question 10 in a minute. Right now some of you may be wondering exactly what an 'explicit need' is and whether you have one or not.

Back in the 1970's Neil Rackham conducted the largest to date research study of successful selling engagements for Xerox and IBM. Rackham's team of 30 researchers studied the dynamics of 35,000 sales calls. The research and analysis took 12 years to complete after which Rackham published the groundbreaking classic SPIN® Selling (McGraw-Hill, 1988). Here again, highly recommended reading. You would be doing yourself a favor to invest in both SPIN Selling as well as the follow-up book, The SPIN Selling Fieldbook.

The ground breaking discovery Rackham made in his research was this. The greatest differentiating factor between the top successful sales reps and the rest of the crowd is their ability to conduct effective needs analysis that leads to explicit needs. Effective needs analysis requires that we ask incisive questions to uncover explicit needs. Rackham's **SPIN** Selling model facilitates this process. **S**ituational questions point to **P**roblem questions that point to **I**mplication questions that point to Needs/Payoff questions (hence the **SPIN** acronym). When the **SPIN** model is executed efficiently the result is either an explicit need, or an implied need. Explicit needs point to urgency for a solution while implied needs point to complacency in making a purchase decision. An explicit need indicates that the need is so great, if a solution is not implemented the repercussions will have dire consequences or, at a minimum, an unacceptable outcome. Here's a true story example.

Paul was a colleague of mine back in the mid 90's when I worked for a small hi-tech company in Atlanta. Paul was our European sales manager. Paul loved to play tennis. One day, after playing a few sets, Paul didn't feel so well. Nothing serious he thought, "I'll just take a couple aspirin and lay down for a while." In Paul's mind his condition was not serious at all; just a few aspirin and some rest will do the trick. In other words, inactivity on Paul's part wouldn't be the end of the world; no dire consequences, no unacceptable outcome. Paul's level of need at that point would be what Rackham calls an 'implied need'. "It would be nice if I felt better but there's no need to check myself into the hospital for Pete's sake." Now at this point, if I were a heart surgeon trying to sell Paul on a few days in the Hospital for some open heart surgery I would have a tough job on my hands. Fast forward a few days. A bunch of aspirin and more rest and guess what? Paul still doesn't feel so well. Guess what else? Paul still feels like its no big deal.

Of course Paul's wife begins to think otherwise. Finally, after much cajoling, Paul's wife gets him to visit the doctor. The doctor takes some history and a few x-ray's. Uh oh! Things look a little abnormal. Paul begins to get nervous. Suddenly all that aspirin and laying down doesn't seem like it was such a good idea. An EKG and a stress test and things look even more troubling. The sense of urgency is now really starting to build. Finally the doctor performs an angiogram and the results are conclusive. "Mr. Paul," says his physician, "I must inform you that you are in desperate need of a triple bypass my friend." Suddenly, Paul's previously implied need of "it would be nice to feel better" turned into a very compelling and explicit need of "please save my life as soon as possible!" Paul indeed did have open heart surgery within the next 72 hours. Happily, all went well, and Paul returned to good health.

My hope is that, after completing the call activity exercise over the past five days, you have discovered that you have a very compelling, urgent and explicit need to change your call activity habits. Am I comparing the importance of your call activity to the life threatening condition of heart disease? In terms of real life health and well being, absolutely not. In terms of your real professional life health and well being, absolutely yes! Which means you now should understand that if you do nothing to improve your call activity, there will be dire consequences over the horizon (question 7 of the burning-platform questionnaire). OK then, all my call activity bypass patients, read on. To all you others, good luck with the ticking time bomb you are carrying around in your empty Outlook calendars.

Quest *for* **Success Directive #8:**
If it's not in your schedule, it's not real. Plan to win!
Schedule Everything!

"Don't Do This!"

On to burning-platform question 10; what are you going to do about it? Remember the one about the patient who walks into the doctor's office shaking his arm saying "Doctor, It hurts when I do this". The doctor offers the obvious advice, as he mimics the patient's shaking arm, "Stop doing this." The stop doing this approach would mean you identify all non-selling activities and simply stop doing them. Obviously, there are some non-customer selling activities you cannot eliminate completely. However, there are surely things you are doing that you can, and should, simply stop doing. Here's a good example.

I had a rep in Miami named Joe. Joe was a classic case of someone who was doing things that were clearly not his job or responsibility. After Joe sold a system, he always made it a point to visit with the customer during the installation process. I think this is absolutely the right thing to do. When a customer invests tens of thousands of dollars in your product, you owe them the courtesy of a visit during delivery and installation. However, Joe's problem was he hung around too long. Every install of sophisticated equipment is going to have some problems, and in some cases serious problems. When this happened, Joe would make the mistake of allowing himself to get sucked into the black hole of customer service. Because Joe was a successful sales rep he had a lot of installs. Consequently, he spent a great deal of his time trying to solve problems during the install and ramp up time directly following installation. In fact, Joe was spending up to 25% of his time in this exercise. When I asked Joe why he was doing this he simply told me that if he didn't, no one else would.

Joe had fallen prey to the hero/martyr syndrome; a self perpetuating cycle that was sapping 25% of valuable selling time out of his week. The insidiousness of Joe's situation was the more he helped out his customers after the sale, the more the technicians and the customer service organization allowed him to do so. Joe became an enabler. "Hey, if Joe's going to help us out, we'll let him help us out all he wants!" How about you? Got a bit of the hero/martyr syndrome cooking in your selling life right now? It's time to look at your five days of activity and weed out those things which you have no business doing.

Now, if you are engaged in some hero/martyr activities just dropping them cold turkey may create some problems. Don't do the right thing and in the process hurt yourself, your company and your customers. Make sure you hand off those responsibilities in a professional way. What Joe in Miami needed to do was visit his customer during install and ensure them that if problems arose, there was an entire organization of professionals in customer service and support who were available to do their jobs and address the issues. In fact, here are their names and numbers. Your role in these potential black hole situations is defined in success directive #9 below.

Quest *for* Success Directive #9:

Stop engaging in activities that are clearly not your job or your responsibility. Just say NO! Be professional.

Be a Facilitator, Not a Fixer!

Pay Yourself First

OK then, back to what else are you going to do about how and where you are spending your time? Many of the activities you are engaging in every week are your job and responsibility. They are essential, and you can't delegate them to others. Things like reporting in your CRM, paperwork and administration functions, generating proposals, business development activities, etc. And let's not forget some of the other huge drains on our time for those of us working in large corporate environments; answering 50 to 100 e-mails a day as well as endless conference calls and webinars. How can we free up our time when we've got all this 'stuff' in our way?

This is actually a really simple fix ladies and gentlemen, and it comes in two parts. Of course what I mean by simple is it's simple to explain, not as simple to do.

Part 1: Do what our sales manager friend Sean in Australia does. Schedule everything. Now that you have the benefit of seeing where you are really spending your time after the five-day activities exercise, and you have a compelling and explicit need to change, you should be chomping at the bit to schedule your time with worthwhile activities. Take out a sheet of paper or open up your task list in Outlook, and get ready to make a list of the activities you need to accomplish over the next five business-days. We're going to go through several iterations here, so don't worry too much about the order; just get everything you plan to do over the next five days on the list.

Part II: How many times have you heard the expression 'it's a matter of priorities'? Now we're going to apply what some people call the golden rule of wealth building, which by the way is the reason we're in sales in the first place, to build wealth, right? It's called 'Pay Yourself First'. We need to make this rule our number one priority when it comes to scheduling our activities. As sales professionals, we get paid when we sell. Therefore, paying ourselves first means our number one priority should be making sales calls. Remember we said that making sales calls is a 'categorical imperative'. That means regardless of the circumstances, this imperative applies. By the way, when we sell something it's not only good for us, it's good for our company as well. So, paying ourselves first is good for everyone in the food chain. I'm sure your sales manager would agree with this logic.

Let's go back to your planner and your Outlook and get ready to plan the next five days business days. Start by paying yourself first and scheduling your sales calls. Most of us have performance standards we are expected to meet in terms of call activity. This may include phone calls and/or face-to-face meetings. For some of you out in the field it may be 20 face-to-face appointments per week. For others on the phones it may be 80 calls per day. Let's say you are expected to make 20 face-to-face calls per week. If you are like most sales reps, you are probably averaging less than 15. So how many calls do you think you should put into your new schedule? Bingo! At least 20! Let's not start out on the wrong foot and schedule only 15 calls. That's just planning to fail. If your performance standard is 20 calls, then schedule a minimum of 20 calls. Of course, some calls will get cancelled, and some others may pop up. The point is you need to begin your schedule with at least 20 customer selling engagements.

Now, let's go back to your task list. Before you schedule any other tasks, go through and eliminate any activities that are not your job, or your responsibility. That's right. Just say no! Hand the ball over to whoever owns it. Stop playing the hero/martyr. Now, take the rest of your activities, and schedule them on your five-day calendar in the time you have left. Uh oh! There's not enough time in the week! Welcome to the pro's my friend. There is never enough time! Never! Guess what? I just lied. Time for another Rules of the Road sign.

Rules of the Road

There Is Always Enough Time For Sales Calls

There Is Never Enough Time For The Other Stuff

Quest *for* **Success Directive #10:**
Make a list, just say no.
Pay Yourself First!

It truly is a matter of priorities. Pay yourself first, and there will always be enough time for sales calls. As for the rest of the stuff you need to do, you need to figure out how you're going to get it done. Here are a couple strategies for you.

Prioritize:

Do you remember the sub-title to this section of the book? **Busy Work or Busy Working?** Why is it that busy work, work that really should have a low priority in our schedules, gets elevated to the very top of the list of things to do? Two reasons. First, by definition, busy work makes us feel like we're...well, busy. Which in turn makes us feel like we're actually doing something of value. Never mind the fact that what we're doing is irrelevant to the moment; we're busy, and we're getting something done! Number two, busy work is easy to do. Taking two hours to run across town to buy a toner cartridge for your home office printer at 10:00 am on Monday morning is a lot easier than locking yourself in your office at 8:00 am and dialing-for-dollars for four hours of business development calls to customers who usually don't want to talk to you anyway. Besides, when they say they don't want to see you, what do you say? Who needs the rejection? It's much easier to hop in the car, drive across town and stop along the way for a latte and a muffin at Starbuck's while you're at it.

Time to get back to your task list and be honest with yourself. Get the busy work off your list and out of your schedule. De-prioritize it to another time and place, or better yet eliminate it completely. Order your ink cartridges on line, have them delivered, make your own coffee and skip the muffin altogether. I think I see another road sign ahead followed by your next strategy for getting things done.

Delegate:

In my experience, delegating is one of the toughest things for us sales folks to handle. It's my account so I need to do everything, right? Again, the hero/martyr syndrome creeps in and weighs us down with too many tasks and responsibilities. In reality, the most successful sales professionals are not hoarders of responsibility, they are masters at delegating and poaching. They delegate tasks and poach on resources, even when those resources don't belong to them. They are the ones who get everyone around them working on their stuff. You don't see them running and rushing around or breaking a sweat, even in times of crisis. Instead they are cool, calm and, most important, in command of their surroundings and the situation. When something blows up and everyone else is wringing their hands or losing their heads, you see them pick up their cell phones, get a hold of so-and-so and what's-their-name, calmly explain the situation, get a commitment for action, hang up the phone and then order another latte.

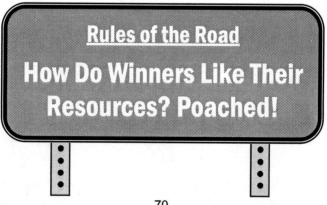

Rules of the Road

How Do Winners Like Their Resources? Poached!

You probably have a wonderful support team around you ready, willing, and able to help you; and there they sit. You don't call, you don't write... You're too busy doing everything yourself playing the hero/martyr.

Let's get back to your task list. How many activities can you delegate to your support team, poach on other resources, and get done quickly? Hey! Stop being greedy and pick some! "But Dave, I'm the only one who can do it." Time for another object lesson. It's perfectly Okay to say "No one can do it like me". It's totally unacceptable to say "No one else can do it *but* me." If you really think no one can do it *but* you, then there are a few psychologists I would refer you to so they can talk to you about something they call the Messiah Complex.

Now, get the list out, and start delegating as many tasks as you can. Your goal is to reduce personally involved activities down to a few phone calls for help and support. Your calendar around your 20 scheduled sales calls should now be freeing up a bit in terms of the other 'stuff' you need to get done.

However, you probably still don't have enough time to get everything done; right? Here's the final strategy.

Make Time:

Some people say you can't save time, you can only spend it. Meaning, you will choose to spend time on doing this thing or that thing. In either case, you are spending time, and time and tide keep moving on. However, you can make time. Here's where we separate the 'going the extra milers' from the 'walk a mile and that's it crowd'. I have never been in a sales role, or managed a sales team where everything that needed to get done could get done in 40 cycles (hours) per week. If you have activities that are a priority, that can not be delegated, and cannot get done between 9 to 5, Monday thru Friday, you have got to make time to do them by adding to your 40 cycles and not reprioritizing what is already in your schedule; your selling time. If that means evenings of work, instead of Monday Night Football or Must See TV, then so be it. If that means weekends spent on tasks not yet completed instead of golf, boating, hoarse back riding or what ever you do on weekends, then so be it. In my mind this is the job you signed up for, and for those of us who signed on to sell for a living, it *always* requires more than 40 cycles to be successful.

Now, there is one profound exception to this rule; family. For example, I would always go to my kid's high school music concert before I got caught up on my CRM. I wouldn't miss the concert, and that meant I would be up late that night doing my CRM afterwards. I know all too well that I need to be careful here. You fellow road warriors know what I am talking about. In my sales career, I have left many precious things behind on the road that are never coming back to me. I made choices, and I am still living with the consequences of some of them. The key here my friends is priorities and balance. Perhaps a story about Vince Lombardi illustrates this best.

Vince Lombardi was the new head football coach for the Green Bay Packers. It was just before his first game as coach, and it was time for him to come into the locker room and speak to the team. You know, the Knut Rockne motivational stuff. Time was quickly passing by and no Coach Lombardi. The players started to wonder what was going on. Then, with just three minutes left before they would run onto the field, Coach Lombardi came out to address the team. Silently he paced back and forth while he stared at them. Finally he said the following words. "Gentlemen, we will be successful this year if you can focus on three things and three things only. Your family, your religion and the Green Bay Packers." What followed in terms of the success of the Green Bay Packers and Coach Lombardi is historic. Focus on your family, your faith and your business. Understand that the health and wellbeing of all three are closely tied together, and I know you'll make the right decisions about what and when to add to your 40 cycles as well as what high school music concerts you don't want to miss.

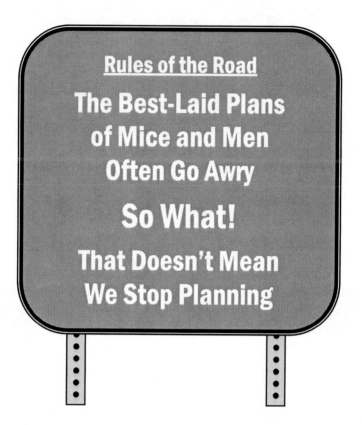

If your first scheduled week goes precisely as planned, it will be a miracle! Let me tell you now it's not going to happen. If you schedule 20 sales calls, you may make only 15. On the other hand, you may make 25. The sales playing field is dynamic, and things can change rapidly. However, that doesn't mean that your plan is not working, and it certainly doesn't mean you should stop planning. Planning your schedule may have seemed difficult, but believe me, that was the easy part.

Executing your schedule according to schedule is the hard part. So again, let me offer you two simple coaching tips.

1. You should be driving the schedule. The schedule should not be driving you. It's the difference between managing your business and allowing the business to manage you. Take control! Keep it! Stay on schedule!

2. Changes to the schedule must be filtered through your scheduling criteria:

   - Do not engage in activities that are not your job or your responsibility – You are a facilitator, not a fixer.

   - Pay yourself first. Schedule your sales calls before everything else.

   - Everything in the schedule is prioritized, including changes to the schedule.

   - Delegate and poach as much as possible.

   - Make time when possible.

   - Focus on family, faith, company.

Quest *for* **Success Directive #11:**

"Your family, your religion, and the Green Bay Packers."

Prioritize! Delegate! Make Time!

Now, If You Really Want This To Work...

There's always one more thing isn't there? Yes. If you really want this to work, you're going to have to do one more thing. Get an accountability partner. Many years ago, whenever my ex-mother-in-law, God rest her soul, would hear me start to talk about what I was *going* to do, she would quickly interrupt me with these endearing words of encouragement, "The road to hell is paved with good intentions." Right, thanks a lot mom!

I'm sure you have great intentions for your new schedule. However, without the element of accountability, it's going to be real easy to opt out at the first sign of difficulty. So, you need someone to keep you accountable. Someone you share your calendar with who will hold you accountable to your promises and check on your progress. In my view, your best accountability partner will be your manager. Send them your calendar and then schedule a 15 minute phone call to review and discuss. By the way, I would love to be a fly on the wall to see the look of astonishment on your manager's face when they get the e-mail with your calendar attached along with your request for a phone call to review. At the end of the following week, send them your new calendar, get on the phone for 15 minutes and discuss what happened last week and what's going to happen the coming week. Be sure to stick to the scheduling criteria we established in this chapter.

Once you start this process you may just be surprised at the support you get from your manager for dismissing the things that are not your job, as well as help in the areas of delegating and resource poaching.

If you are part of a sales team, be prepared for some potential hate mail from your colleagues who will very likely be required by your manager to do the same thing with their schedules. Hey, before you know it you may even start to see an improvement in the relationship you have with your manager. "Who is this person? I used to feel like my manager was working against me. Now they're my advocate!" Trust me, lots of good things will start to happen. Most importantly, do this for one month and you will have developed a habit.

Quest *for* **Success Directive #12:**
The road to hell is paved with good intentions.
Get an Accountability Partner!

Let's finish up Step 2, **Sales** Activity, with some action items.

Quest *for* Success Directives

#6 *Your categorical imperative:*
      Make more sales calls!

#7 *Stop waiting in line for success*
      – Take the stairs!

#8 *Don't fail to plan, plan to win!*
      Schedule everything!

#9 *Be a Facilitator, not a Fixer!*

#10 *Pay yourself first!*

#11 *Focus on 3 things: Prioritize,*
      Delegate, Make Time!

#12 *Stay off the road to hell –*
      Get an accountability partner!

Step 3:

Get Smart & Sell!

Qualified Activity
QuikTrip or Quick Print?

In the late 90's, I was a regional sales director working for a company headquartered in the northeast. We primarily sold into the quick-print market; companies such as Kinko's, Minute Man Press, Quick Copy and Alphagraphics to name a few. Our products included digital printing systems designed for commercial use. At that time, and to this day, there is a very successful gas station/convenience store chain in the southeast called QuikTrip. (In my view the very best in the business in terms of quality and customer service.) OK Dave, quick printers and gas stations; what's the point? Here it is.

Back in Step 2, **Get Busy... Sales Activity**, our emphasis was on making enough sales calls to meet performance expectations. For example, if your company's performance standard is 20 face-to-face calls per week, then making 20 sales calls per week is your categorical imperative. If it is 40 calls per week then 40 is the imperative. However, nowhere in Step 2 did we talk about making *qualified* calls. Meaning, calls to the right kinds of customers; companies that fit squarely in our selling space. Here's the quick printers and QuickTrip analogy I used back then with my team to illustrate the point.

"OK team, you're making 20 calls per week. Great! The question is; are you calling on QuikTrip's or Quick Printers? Obviously a gas station/convenience store such as QuikTrip does not fit the profile of a customer in the market for a digital printing system. QT is a retail business that sells gas and convenience items to the general public. We should be calling on customers that fit our target profile; namely quick printers with annual revenues of at least $1,000,000 and above. However, if you guys actually did spend some of your time calling on QT convenience stores there's a remote possibility that after making enough calls you might hear one of the counter clerks say; "Hey, we certainly don't need any printing equipment here at QuikTrip. However, my brother-in-law is a printer and he happens to be in the market for some new equipment. Here's his phone number." It's not probable, but it could happen. Here's my point. I am using QuickTrip as an analogy for prospects in the printing market that *do not* fit our target profile. We absolutely should be calling on prospects that *do* fit squarely in our selling space; quick printers.

By the way, don't ever let me see a real QuickTrip on a call report."

Remember, Step 2 is Sales Activity; Step 3 is Qualified Activity. By the way, once you complete Step 2 and begin sharing your calendar with your manager I'm sure you will soon have all of the QuikTrip's purged from your schedule.

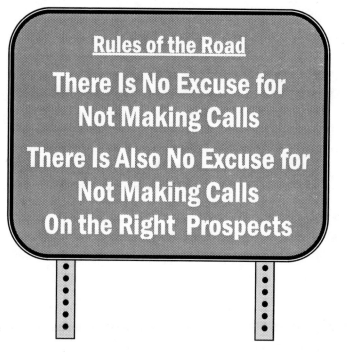

Rules of the Road

There Is No Excuse for Not Making Calls

There Is Also No Excuse for Not Making Calls On the Right Prospects

Quest *for* **Success Directive #13:**
Activity for activity's sake is a waste of valuable time.
Engage in Qualified Activity!

Who Should We Be Calling On?

In my previous example, our market was primarily quick printers. At that time there were about 30,000 quick printers in the US. That doesn't mean that all 30,000 were viable prospects for us. Some of them were QuikTrip's disguised as quick printers. Our printing systems cost anywhere from $200,000 to over $500,000. In fact, at the time the average annual revenue for the 30,000 quick printers in the US was about $400,000. How hard do you think it would be for a business with $400,000 in annual revenues to get financing for a $300,000 piece of equipment? Exactly! Just about impossible. In our experience, we needed to be calling on companies with revenues of at least $1,000,000 per year and higher; and most importantly profitably. Even multi-million dollar businesses can't obtain funding to purchase equipment if they're losing money.

So how did we differentiate the $1,000,000+ businesses from the rest? How were we able to determine how much revenue a company was doing when they were a small business and not publicly traded? After all we couldn't just go on-line and look at their annual report. Again, our experience in the market showed that in the printing business each employee represented approximately $125,000 in annual revenue for that business. Okay, so that means a qualified quick print business for us would have to have at least 8 employees; 10

and above would be even better. Now we're starting to narrow the field and weed out the QuikTrips. After all, if we spent time calling on quick printers with 5 employees or less, we would have done just as well calling on the QuikTrip convenience stores; neither one is a qualified prospect.

You may have hundreds, or even thousands, of prospects in your market. The customer qualifying criteria graph below illustrates the three segmentations of customers within your market in relation to where you should be investing your time.

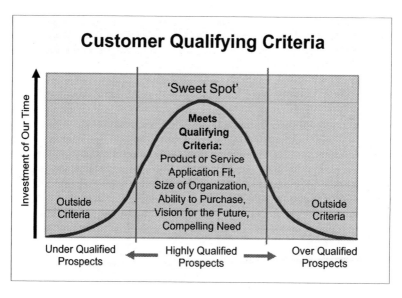

The segment on the left represents under qualified customers who do not meet the threshold of your customer qualifying criteria. As in my example above, calling on printers with less than 8 to 10 employees would not have been a wise investment of our time.

These companies simply would not be able to afford our product.

The segment on the right represents over qualified customers who exceed your criteria. For example, I have a client that manufactures and markets industrial grade impact wrenches for assembly line applications. Their customers are the likes of GM and Whirlpool. Let's say you worked for a company that manufactured power wrenches for the consumer market; the weekend do-it-yourselfers. You sell to big box retailers such as Home Depot and Lowes. If you decided to call on GM, you would definitely be selling outside your sweet spot according to our customer qualifying criteria graph. As good as your power tools may be for consumers, they could not begin to meet the performance demands of an industrial assembly line.

The center of the bell curve in our graph tells us where we should be investing our time. The farther away you get from the 'Sweet Spot' in the center, the less time you should be spending with those customers. When we stray outside of the 'Sweet Spot', we are selling outside our space, and our chances for success are substantially diminished.

Quest *for* **Success Directive #14:**
Selling outside of your space diminishes sales success.
Sell In Your Sweet Spot!

Customer Qualifying Criteria:
The Profile of The Ideal Prospect

So what does the profile of your ideal prospect look like? You may be saying there is no such thing as an ideal prospect; we sell to all kinds of customers. Okay, I'll grant you that. If you sell a broad line of products or services you are correct. However, for each specific product or service you are selling, there is an ideal prospect that can be qualified using specific criteria such as: the size of the company, the type of business, the level of revenue and profitability, the market or sector they service, the product and/or service offering, the types of processes and applications they employ, their people, and even their culture and philosophy. These are just some of the metrics you can apply to the customer qualifying criteria to determine where your sweet spot is. Your company may already have a set of highly formalized qualifying criteria, or perhaps they're just sending you out into the world looking for warm bodies. Certainly, warm bodies are exactly what we're after. However, *qualified* warm bodies is the criteria we need to apply.

When we have a well defined set of customer qualifying criteria for our product or service, we have defined our 'Sweet Spot' for selling. If we're fishing for bass, we need to start by fishing in a bass pond rather than a trout stream. Therefore, precisely defining what a qualified customer looks like is vitally important to our success. The old expression, "everyone is a prospect" may sound good, but it is certainly not a good strategy for sales effectiveness.

Here's a more accurate saying I heard when I was a young adult, and I certainly offer this sound advice to my of-age children. "Don't date someone you wouldn't marry." Meaning, if the person you are dating does not have the qualities of someone you would marry (they don't meet your criteria for a mate), why waste your time dating them? In the end you'll probably split up or worse, make a terrible mistake in marrying someone you are not compatible with. Therefore, don't engage in the sales process with a customer who does meet your customer qualifying criteria. In the end, the odds are you will likely go your separate ways without closing the deal. So, why waste your time in the first place? Well, because he or she is so pretty and good looking! In other words, they're such a big account, they're so attractive as a customer, they even have a marbled lobby. How could we not call on them? Pretty, attractive and good looking is like beauty; it's only skin deep. Don't be blinded by the lights. Unless there is the substance of tangible qualifying criteria you have literally "no business" engaging with unqualified accounts.

The qualifying criteria in the center sweet spot on our graph should at a minimum include the following.

• **Product or Service Application Fit**

Your product or service is appropriate for the customer's application. Don't try and sell commercial grade power wrenches, meant for the weekend do-it-yourselfer, into an industrial application like the assembly line at GM.

• **Size of Organization**

Based on their size, purchasing your product or service is within the financial means of the company. Too small may mean not enough revenue to obtain financial approval for your product or service.

• **Ability to Purchase**

In terms of credit standing the customer has the financial wherewithal to purchase. Even though the organization may be big enough in terms of revenue, they may not have the financial strength to purchase. Those of us who sell products that require financing know all too well about the dreaded low Paydex. Paydex is a D&B rating indicating a company's ability to pay their debts on time, based on their payment history. For example, a Paydex of 90 to 100 indicates that the company has a very good history of paying their monthly bills well within payment terms, usually 30 days. You would feel very good about extending credit to a company with a Paydex in the 90's. On the other hand, a company with a Paydex of 60 indicates that as a creditor, you will likely have to wait 22 days beyond payment terms to receive payment, or 52 days total. What do you think would happen to you if you were continually 22 days late with every mortgage payment? You get the picture. No matter how big the company may be, a low Paydex score will likely mean a very slim chance of that customer obtaining financing for your product or service. By the way, if you sell a service, your accounting department is going to look at your customer's Paydex to determine if they can meet payment requirements. Again, if the Paydex is low, the probability of getting your customer credit approved will also be low. In my experience, the ability of a company to purchase is always a huge problem for sales reps to understand and get their heads around. "Hey, I signed up this huge customer! They want to do business with us. But, the people in accounting will not approve them. What's up with that?!" That's easy. Your customer does not have the ability to purchase because they are a bad credit risk.

- **Vision for the Future**

The customer has specific business initiatives in place for continued growth and success vs. a wait-and-see strategy. In the next section I'll tell you all about customers with no vision.

- **Compelling Need**

  The customer's current situation is creating a need that is extremely urgent. As a result, they are compelled to take action in order to avoid what will be an unacceptable outcome or dire consequence for inactivity. Remember my friend Paul in Step 2 with the heart condition. Prior to examination by his physician, Paul felt his need was clearly less than compelling; pop some aspirin and take it easy. However, after thorough testing the need became very compelling when the results indicated Paul needed bypass surgery, immediately! Paul quickly understood he had an extremely compelling need that if not addressed would lead to a dire consequence and unacceptable outcome; his death!

On the following page, take a few minutes to list and define your customer qualifying criteria. I have included the five we have talked about here. For each category include specific numbers to quantify the criteria. Be as specific as possible with the categories and the quantifiers. Of course, your Customer Qualifying Criteria will be unique to the product or service you are selling. Be sure to add as many 'other' categories as appropriate.

Product or Service Application Fit:

Size of Organization:

Ability to Purchase:

Vision for the Future:

Compelling Need:

Other:

Now comes the fun part. Send your completed list of Customer Qualifying Criteria to your manager for feedback and validation. Again, I would love to be a fly on the wall when he or she reads your e-mail. A few e-mails and iterations later, and I know you will have a well-defined list of Customer Qualifying Criteria.

Quest *for* Success Directive #15:
Everyone is *not* a prospect.
Real Prospects Meet
Your Customer Qualifying Criteria!

Okay, so now we are at least calling on customers within our 'Sweet Spot' who meet our customer qualifying criteria and have the wherewithal to purchase our product, if interested. Right? Great! Hold on a second, what about that little 'if interested' part? Yes, I slipped that in here almost under the radar. The truth is, on the radar screen, the 'if interested' qualification may seem like a small blip, but in reality this criteria is like a stealth bomber. You can't see it, but it's a huge deadly aircraft flying in to carpet bomb your success, and possibly your career in the process. How do we see beyond the stealth to determine the 'if interested' factor? Well, the ability to do just that is a very effective and highly specialized skill that successful sales professionals have refined into a keenly developed sense; a sixth-sense in fact.

"I See Dead People"

Okay Dave, now you're starting to freak me out; "I see dead people"? Yes. The question is; do you?

From our customer's perspective, there are two iterations of 'if interested'. One speaks to vision, and the other to choice. When a customer has no vision for their business, either because they are afraid to make a decision to move forward, or they are simply mired in complacency, they will have little or no interest in purchasing. On the other hand, when a customer has a vision for their business they are committed to action; they are going to make a purchase decision with someone. However, until you outsell your competition, they may not yet be interested in purchasing from you. "I see dead people" relates to the former condition. We will deal with the customer's choice to purchase from you in later chapters.

"Houston, We Have a Problem."

A few years back, I was starting a brand new job as a sales manager, again in the Southeast. My first trip into the field was to Houston. I had planned to spend two days traveling with our local sales rep, Ed. When Ed picked me up at the airport, my heart jumped with both excitement and relief. You know, the kind of situation where you wipe the sweat off your forehead and say "wheww". You sales managers know what I'm talking about. Meeting one of your reps for the first time is kind of like a blind date. You've heard good things about them, but until you see them face-to-face you're filled with anxiety. Will they present themselves as a professional, or look like someone who keeps their suit in the glove compartment of their car? Remember the book *Dress for Success*? Appearance really does count. Thank goodness, Ed looked like a CEO! He was middle-aged (with a touch of grey hair), nice suit and tie, polished shoes, the whole package. Then Ed greeted me and I was even more assured. Ed was extremely poised and professional. I know I shouldn't be biased, because I once worked with a guy who sounded like a New York City cab driver but guess what; he was our division's top sales performer. Of course, his territory was Manhattan.

I got into Ed's SUV, and off we went to make calls. We pulled up to our first account, a quick printer, walked through the front door, and that's when the walls quickly 'came a tumbling down'. That's right, even Joshua himself could not have survived the battle I was going to be fighting for the next day and a half.

First of all, it was about 9:30 am and the customer's office was deadly quiet. Not a good sign for a business that should be filled with the sound of running printing equipment. Second, it was a very small office. My guess was no more that half a dozen employees; certainly not a qualified prospect according to our 8 to 10 or more employee qualifying criteria. Shortly, the owner came out, greeted us, shook hands, and then firmly held his ground in the lobby rather than invite us into his office to talk. That was the third indication I was in the freefall stage of a crash and burn sales call. "You know," he started out, "the market is really tough right now. I don't see us making any equipment purchases for the foreseeable future." As he spoke he slowly shook his head back and fourth in a demonstrative no-way, no-how gesture of negativity just in case, I suppose, we might not be comprehending his words. Trust me; the message was all too clear. The rest of the day was filled with variations on the theme with a few: "Oh, Mr. Jones? He's not here. Did you have an appointment? I'll let him know you called…" thrown in for good measure. That evening, I called my wife and told her I had probably made the biggest mistake of my career in coming to work for this company. I also told her that, while I thought Ed looked like a top sales rep, he really was the Devil sent to torment and punish me for all my past selling sins of not making enough sales calls and over aggressive discounting. "Really honey, he looks like a man, but he's really Satan."

Day 2 was Groundhog Day; more of the same. Unlike the Bill Murray classic, this wasn't at all funny. I had scheduled 2 hours with Ed on the way to the airport to review our time together. So, to this point I had made no comments. I suppose I was hoping for at least one good call to have something positive to talk about. Finally, on our very last call, we pulled up to a nice sized office building with a large sign on the façade. Now we're talking I thought. There must be 50 to 100 people working here. We walked into the lobby and announced ourselves to the receptionist. As we waited to see the owner, I noticed something on the table. It was a newsletter published by the printing company. In the newsletter, there were a number of articles on what was going on at So-&-So Printing. There was an article profiling the new sales rep they had just hired. And another on the latest equipment they had just added which would allow them to offer expanded quality services to their customers. "Hallelujah!" Finally a customer who isn't holed up in their bunker waiting for a bomb to fall on their heads, hoping it isn't a bunker-buster that finally puts them out of their misery and out of business!

We met the president in his nicely appointed office. Immediately he began to tell us about how his business was experiencing continual and steady growth, and, how he was targeting new markets and customers for the coming year. He elaborated on the aggressive but studied plans he had to grow his business, followed by some of the material issues he would have to resolve in order to reach his objectives. "Which is why" he continued, "I wanted to meet with you folks. Maybe you can help me." Suddenly this customer appeared to have a radiant golden halo hovering over his head and the room began to fill with a heavenly light. I looked over to Ed and saw that his cheeks had plumped up and turned a bright cherub red. And, he was strumming a little golden harp which emanated the sweetest angelic music as he floated above his chair. Had I died and gone to heaven? Was this customer an angel sent from above to save me? Was Ed not really the Devil after all? "Well Ed, why don't you tell Mr. So-&-So how we can mitigate the issues he has shared with us and help him achieve his objectives." Guess what? Ed performed like a star, and I managed to avoid retribution for yet another day. Sorry Satan.

We stopped at Starbuck's on the way to the airport to debrief our 1-1/2 day's selling activities. "I'll be honest Ed. Last night I thought I had made the biggest mistake of my career coming to work for this company. And, I was completely convinced that you were the Devil incarnate. However, you really saved the day with that last call." Actually, I didn't tell Ed I thought he was the Devil, but I think he got the picture I was painting. I then asked Ed if he had seen the movie *Sixth Sense*. He said he had. I asked if he remembered what the troubled little boy told Bruce Willis. "Sure,' Ed replied, 'I see dead people.'" "Guess what?" I told Ed, "You don't!" Ed sat straight up in his chair in surprise. I think he wanted to defend himself, but, since this was our very first meeting, he instead asked me what I meant. I began to go through the procession of customers we had visited for the first day and a half. All of them holed up in their bunkers waiting for something outside their control to change; the economy, customer confidence, credit constraints, an upturn in business, a miraculous turn around of some sort, etc, etc. "Ed, not a single one of those customers had a vision for their business" I said. "They have no plans for their future. No idea of the real issues they are facing. No newsletter! In fact, they're just holding on for dear life. They are the walking dead! You walk in to see them and there they are standing right in front of you, three feet from your face, dead as can be, and you can't see it. You can't see dead people Ed!" "Okay…" was all Ed said. Perhaps he was waiting for some redeeming words to surface in the conversation. "However Ed, that last call was heaven. In fact, that last call we just made was exactly what I am talking about. Mr. So-&-So is alive and well and a really good prospect for us." Finally Ed started to nod his head in approval and smile a bit. "Ed, you need to learn how to see dead people and when you do, run as fast as you can to your next prospect. Stop wasting your valuable time with customers who have no vision of the future for their business, and start investing time with customers who are alive and well and have real plans for success."

Well then the flood gates opened and Ed let it all out. He told me how unhappy he had become in his job with no customers seeming to be interested in his products. He told me how he had previously been very successful but lately he was in a rut he couldn't seem to explain. "You know Dave, you are 100% right. I am wasting my time with people who aren't prospects at all. Dead people! Starting right now I'm going to start focusing on customers like we just called on; the Mr. So-&-So's of the world." Ed and I spent the rest of our time together talking about our next steps for our new found angel, Mr. So-&-So.

Fast forward six months later. Ed had become one of my top reps. During one phone call I remember Ed telling me the following: "Dave, I am having the time of my life right now. I'm selling, I'm happy, and things are going just great." I had four out of eight reps make President's Club that year including Ed. There was no one I was happier for or prouder of than Ed.

Rules of the Road
CAUTION!
Dead People Ahead!
Avoid Like the Plague!

Ed was one of the most unique reps I have ever managed for this reason. I had the 'I see dead people' conversation with Ed just one time on the second day we met, and that's all it took. Ed just flat out ran with it! From a management and coaching perspective that is highly unusual. How about you? Seen any dead people lately?

Where are you investing your time?

Back to our bass pond fishing trip. Okay, so we're at the bass pond instead of the trout stream and we cast in our line. How do we know the bass are going to bite? Obviously the bait must be attractive or we're going to spend all day on the water and leave with nothing but a sun burn and bunch of mosquito bites. We need to be attacking our sweet spot with a product and service offering that is irresistible to our customers (ultimately in a way that is more irresistible than our competitors offering). Now we're starting to go beyond customer qualifying criteria, sweet spots or target markets. Now we are beginning to approach the area of real value.

When We Focus On Our Sweet Spot (Prospects That Meet Our Customer Qualifying Criteria), And Effectively Position Our Products And Services In A Way That Clearly Differentiates Us From Our Competition, A Beautiful Thing Starts To Happen.

We Start Wining!

The Value Factor

I call the intersection of customer qualifying criteria and product/service differentiation the Value Factor. The Value Factor provides us with a template for articulating our product and service offering in a way that resonates value in the minds of our target customers.

When we talk about articulating customer value, we begin to define the messaging we should be employing when we engage with our customers in the selling and buying process. That's right, the selling *and* buying process. How many times have you heard the term buying process associated with the sales process? In just about every company I have experience with, the sales organization runs their business according to an established sales process. Step 1: Hand Raise. Step 2: Qualifying. Step 3: Justification, etc., etc. That's what they teach; that's what is integrated into their CRM; that's how they manage their pipelines and forecast; and that's how they run their business. It's no wonder that after having the company's sales process beat into a sales reps heart and soul, when they get in front of a customer their entire message is in the context of their sales process. "Mr./Mrs. Customer, what we hope to accomplish today is a thorough qualifying of you as a bona-fide prospect for our product or service. I would like to ask you a series of questions to determine if you have the interest and wherewithal to ultimately write us a big fat check. If you do have the interest and the money, after this meeting I'll be able to advance you to the next step in the sales process in my CRM. Which will be good for me because then I can get my manager off my back about updating my pipeline. So, why don't we just get started with a canned PowerPoint presentation which I know is going to get you so excited your socks are going to go up and down. Then to top it all off, I'm going to recite the wonderful value proposition our folks in marketing dreamed up, all to the music of Queen's *We Will Rock You!* You can pound your hands and feet right along with us if you're feeling it."

Ladies and gentlemen of the sales profession, trust me, no matter how much effort your marketing department has put into your value proposition, no matter how big a boom box you bring to the meeting, in the eyes of your customer, this is not a unique message. What is a unique message? Well, that's exactly how we start out the next book in our Quest for Success Selling Series.

Series II

Shut Up & Listen... Say 'So What' & Sell!

Let's finish up Step 3, **Sales** Activity, with some action items.

Quest *for* Success Directives

#13 *Activity for activity's sake is a waste of your valuable time - Engage in qualified activity!*

#14 *Selling outside your space puts you in the danger zone - Sell in your sweet spot!*

#15 *Everyone is not a prospect - Real prospects meet your customer qualifying criteria!*

#16 *Work on your 6th Sense - Stop hanging out with dead people!*

Wrap Up:

Stop Whining...
Get Busy...
Get Smart & Sell!

In Series I we introduced the first three steps of **7 Steps for Taking Control of Your Sales Destiny.** In these three steps I have asked you to do a number of things.

- Put away the crying towels and stop blaming everything and everyone else.

- Make a commitment to accept responsibility for your sales performance.

- Hold yourself accountable for your failures.

- Change what you can – *Yourself!*

- Be willing to 'take the stairs'.

- Schedule everything.

- Prioritize, delegate, make time.

- Pay yourself first by scheduling more sales calls.

- Engage in qualified activity.

- Focus on customers who are in your sweet spot.

- Stop hanging out with "dead people".

If you do nothing else in the 7 steps; if you don't go on to read Series II and III; but you diligently execute Steps 1, 2 and 3 in this book, I guarantee you will experience a significant improvement in sales productivity. Of course, my hope is you not only master these first three steps, but you go on to make a quantum leap in productivity by mastering all **7 Steps for Taking Control of Your Sales Destiny.**

QUEST *for* Success Selling Series

Series I

Sales Lead ⓣⓞ Sales Leadership

Doing Your Best Is Not Good Enough.
You Have to Know What to Do.
Then Do Your Best.

Chapter 1

"Doing Your Best Is Not Good Enough. You Have to Know What to Do. Then Do Your Best."

W.E. Deming

Uh-oh! Here's another in-your-face, cut to the bone, convicting statement. However, this one is not from me.

W. E. Deming (1900 – 1993) is known as the father of Total Quality Management (TQM). Deming is most widely known for his work with post-war Japanese industry. Beginning in 1950, Dr. Deming trained hundreds of Japanese engineers, managers, and scholars in statistical process control (SPC) and concepts of quality. His message to Japan's chief executives was elegantly simple: Improving quality will reduce expenses while increasing productivity and market share.

Subsequently, a number of Japanese manufacturers widely applied Deming's techniques and experienced theretofore unheard of levels of quality and productivity. The improved quality combined with lower pricing created new international demand for Japanese products.

Deming's methodologies proved so successful that ultimately the Japanese Union of Scientists and Engineers board of directors established the Deming Prize, similar to the The Malcolm Baldrige National Quality Award awarded here in the US to companies recognized as having achieved major advances in quality improvement. The Deming Prize has exerted an immeasurable influence directly and indirectly on the development of quality control and quality management in Japan. In 1960, the Prime Minister of Japan (Nobusuke Kishi), acting on behalf of Emperor Hirohito, awarded Dr. Deming Japan's Order of the Sacred Treasure, Second Class. The citation on the medal recognizes Deming's contributions to Japan's industrial rebirth and its worldwide success. In other words, when Dr. Deming says, "Doing your best is not good enough. You have to know what to do. Then do your best.", all of us should sit up and listen.

Great Story!

Does This Have Something to Do With the "Our Sales Productivity Stinks!" Comment By The So-Called Experts?

Well, Dr. Deming is not one of the experts who said our sales productivity stinks. However, if he were here today and looked at the numbers and analysis from the 2009 CSO Insights report, that is exactly what he would say. More importantly, Dr. Deming's comment speaks to why our sales productivity stinks. We're all well intended and doing our best. However, the fact is, when it comes to raising sales productivity, the majority of us simply don't know what to do to. OK Dave, them's fighting words! I agree! We should be mad enough to fight about it. The question is, are we mad enough to do something about it?

Almost without exception, every sales manager I have had the opportunity and privilege to work with, work for, or train in one of my sessions was "doing their best" to succeed. Despite these good intentions, according to CSO Insights, doing our best in most cases has been and continues to be "not good enough".

Each year I review the CSO Insights Survey Results and Analysis on Sales Performance Optimization. 2009 marks the 15th annual publishing of the sales effectiveness report. In the survey of over 1,500 firms, CSO collects data on 100+ unique sales performance metrics.

The companies participating in the survey range from 43.2% in the services sector, 35.0% in manufacturing sector, and 21.8% in other sectors. Within these sectors various industries are represented including financial services, software, hardware/technology, professional services-business, and professional services-high tech, etc. (70% of the companies are located in North America). Overall, 60.3% have revenues under $50M, 24.6% with revenues of $50M to $1B, and 15.1% with revenues exceeding $1B.

Let's revisit some of the numbers and analysis from the 2009 CSO Insights Sales Performance Optimization Survey Results and Analysis. For us managers, I have included many more metrics here than in the previous Burning Platform chapter. I have also added my own comments and some questions we should all be asking ourselves.

- **58.8%** of sales reps are meeting or exceeding quota. This number is down from **61.2%** in 2008.

- **20%** of the sales reps are generating **61.5%** of revenues. **80%** are generating just **38.5%** of revenues.

- **85.9**% of companies are achieving revenue targets. This number is down from **88.2%** in the previous year.

Only 58.8% of sales reps are meeting or exceeding quota (41.2% are not). The 80/20 rule indicates the top 20% of reps are contributing on average over 6 times the revenue per sales rep than the lower 80%. As a result, one might think the number of companies achieving revenue targets would be much lower than 85.9%.

Are companies dumbing down their revenue targets to accommodate poor sales performance?

- Annual sales rep voluntary (rep leaves) turnover rate is **15.3%**. Involuntary (rep is let go) turnover is **13.1%**.

- Only **41.4%** of companies employ competency assessment testing as part of the hiring process; **52.3%** do not.

- **45.3%** of companies say their ability to hire reps who succeed at selling is not meeting expectations.

Sales rep turnover is 28.4% while 50% of companies do not test competency for new hires.

Is it any wonder that 45.3% of companies are disappointed in their new hires?

- **52.3%** of sales leads are self-generated by sales reps compared to **40%** in 2005. This number is obviously tracking in the wrong direction.

- **62.8%** of companies said their adherence to a formalized sales process was random to informal despite the fact that **89%** feel that adherence to the sales process has a modest to significant impact on sales performance.

- Only **30%** of companies consistently use the sales methodology taught in sales training.

- **71.4%** of companies have a formalized CRM implementation for sales. However, only **20.2%** say that

CRM has improved win rates. Only **16.1%** say CRM has shortened the sales cycle. And, only **15.8%** say CRM has helped increase revenues.

- Despite the numbers above, **87%** of companies say they do not plan to change their CRM solution.

Over half of the leads sales reps pursue are self generated. Over 60% of companies do not follow a formalized sales process. 70% do not use the process they are taught in sales training. The benefits of a CRM implementation in terms of win rates, shortened sales cycle and increased revenues are acknowledged by barely over 20% of the companies surveyed.

Are we largely leaving sales reps to their own devices, while expecting a level of performance that only 58.8% are capable of meeting? And, what are we doing to change this perpetual problem?

- Only **47.8%** of forecasted deals are won. **30.4%** are lost deals and **21.9%** result in no decision.

- **40.6%** of companies surveyed said their reps ability to understand the customer's buying process needs improvement.

- **44.7%** said their reps ability to sell value and avoid discounting is below expectations.

- Execution of the sales process is only rated as a **22.2%** factor in why deals are won. ROI and business case receives only an **18.9%** contributory rating.

- **68.7%** of the time the reason we lose deals is the competitor's price and terms.

- **56.2%** of companies are not meeting expectations in conducting win/loss reviews.

We don't understand the customer's buying process very well. We don't know how to sell value very well. Since over 60% of companies do not follow a formalized sales process, is it surprising that execution of the sales process is rated as only a 22% factor and ROI's are rated as only an 18.9% factor in why deals are won? Is it even more surprising that 68.7% of the time the deciding factor in win/loss is price and terms? And now for the cherry on top; 56.2% of companies don't really know why they lose or win deals because they do not conduct win/lose reviews.

Is it any wonder why only 47.8% of forecasted deals are won? What forecasting criteria, if any, are we using?

- **46.7%** of companies say their ability to share best practices across the organization is not meeting expectations.

The statistics above indicate that many organizations suffer from a lack of process, structure, discipline and enforceable standards. Consequently, the majority of reps have been left to their own devices and forced to fend for themselves. One can only ask:

Where's Waldo? Where's the beef?
Where are the best practices in these organizations
to share in the first place?

- Approximately **50%** of companies invest an average of **$1,500** in sales training annually per sales rep.

- Regarding training in the areas of sales skills, sales process, the marketplace, justifying the purchase, sales management, and CRM application, approx. **50%** of companies said that the training was not meeting expectations.

Dialogue from a typical sales management meeting: "Hey team, our sales productivity sucks! What should we do? Well, let's fire the bottom 10% of the dead weight we hired a year ago and we'll do some more sales training for the rest of them. Good idea! In fact, let's just make that a policy. Every 6 months we'll fire, hire and train. Good meeting guys."

Conversation in the hallway after the meeting: "Hey, this sales training stuff just ain't working for me. What about you? Me neither. However, we gotta do it, right? Anyway, it takes the spotlight off us. If they don't perform we just say, 'Hey, you guys were trained. It's not our fault you can't sell.' Yeah, right. Fire, hire and train, that's the ticket."

Why do we perpetuate this vicious cycle?
When is management going to stop blaming the sales rep
and take responsibility for the problem?

Back in the days of black and white TV when I was a kid there was a popular show called *This is Your Life*. The host would chronicle the life of famous and not so famous people by way of recordings and live visits from lifelong friends and family. If you are a sales manager, the numbers I just shared with you from CSO Insights are not about someone else on a TV show from another time and place. They're very likely about you! And rather than a nostalgic walk down memory lane, it should read more like a *This is Your Life in Sales Manager's Hell* episode.

So What Do the Numbers Mean?

Let's say we have 100 sales reps, each with a quota assignment of $1M, expected to generate a total of $100M in revenues. Let's say we achieved plan. The CSO Insights findings would indicate that 20 sales reps would have generated $61.5M in revenues, or $3.075M each, or 307% of quota according to the $1M target for each rep. At the same time 80 sales reps would have generated $38.5M in revenues, or $481,250.00 each, or 48% of quota, on average. OK, you made your overall target so what's the big deal? Well, let's apply your team's level of performance to the rest of the organization that surrounds you and see how this would impact productivity.

Let's start with the service organization. Imagine again that we have 100 service techs and 1,000 service incidents per week, or 10 service incidents per week at 2 calls per day scheduled for each technician. Applying the same productivity numbers from the sales side would mean that in reality 20 service techs would be performing 61.5% of the service calls. That is 615 calls per week for 20 techs. Meaning that instead of 2 calls per day these techs would be making 6.15 calls per day each; 307% productivity. Meanwhile, our other 80 techs would only be making a total of 385 calls per week, or .96 calls per day for each technician; only 48% productivity. What if the service tech servicing your customers was one of the 80 who only made .96 calls per day? If each tech was supposed to be making 2 calls per day that would mean that half of your customers in your territory would not be getting service in a timely manner. How happy do you think your customers would be about that? How do you think this would impact you when it comes time to upgrade these unhappy customers? Finally, how good of a reference base of happy customers would you have in your territory to help you sell to new customers?

Let's stay with the operations side of the house for a moment. At 6.15 calls per day for 20% of the techs vs. .96 calls per day for 80%, how long do you think this level of inefficiency in the service organization could be sustained? For that matter, how long could this level of inefficiency be sustained in any operational function of the company: Manufacturing? Logistics? Accounting? I'm sure you would agree, not very long. Again I must ask, why then is this level of inefficiency tolerated and therefore perpetuated in the sales organizations? At least in some of the better run companies there is a growing realization and recognition equivalent to the first step in any 12-step recovery program; admitting there is a problem.

Here is an example. In the fall of 2008, just about one year ago from the time of this writing, I attended a kick-off meeting for a business unit of a Fortune 50 company. The keynote address was delivered by the CEO and Chairman to a ballroom filled with 600+ sales managers. The CEO began his talk by citing sales performance numbers from the previous year, which were very good by the way. He was about 10 minutes into his 45 minute speech when he began to position the challenges ahead for 2009. "Sales performance is critical!" he exclaimed to the crowd. He then paused for dramatic effect: "And I expect everyone in this room to deliver." There was a second dramatic pause, accompanied by a dead silence in the room. Again he said with authoritative directness, "Let me repeat. I expect everyone in this room to deliver." For the third time, he paused and glared out over his reading glasses at the silent assembly, accentuating the full gravity and solemnity of the moment. "OK, I guess we're done here." His sarcasm served to break the silence and in a few moments a quiet nervous laughter emerged from a few corners. "Now let's talk about how we're going to do it." Having made his point, he continued for the remaining 35 minutes.

One of his comments to the assembled 600+ sales managers was this: "I can not understand why we still have sales reps on our payroll who have not sold anything in the past 12 months." As I listened to this amazing statement, I could only imagine how many sales reps were on the payroll who had not sold anything in 9 months, or even 2 straight quarters. "This practice will not continue." he went on to say. After planting this very pointed performance standards steak in the ground, he began to outline his vision and directives for more effective performance management from the team. A Senior VP would follow his keynote with an entire session on how their existing CRM application was being retooled to mirror the customer's buying process. In fact, having first hand experience with this company and their CRM implementation, which by the way was in excess of 15,000 seats, I had a sense that if their current step-of-sale process had not been so deeply ingrained in the company's systems, they would have tossed their entire sales process in the trash can and replaced it with the customer's buying process. The message delivered that day by this CEO was clear.

Poor sales performance is no longer acceptable in this organization.

What Does Service Response Time Have to Do With Our Poor Forecast Accuracy?

In all my years in sales, it has more often than not been the case that when something blows up at the customer site, the sales rep is the first person they call: "Hey Dave, I ordered supplies from your company (all of a sudden I own the company), and they have not been delivered. Now I can't get my work out! What are you going to do about it?" Or, "Hey Dave, we ordered replacement parts from you (now I am the parts and shipping department) 5 days ago, and they're still on backorder. I'm down hard! What are you going to do about it?" Finally, "Hey Dave, remember that service contract you coerced me into signing (now I'm a coercer)? Guess what? That 4-hour response time was up 24 hours ago. What are you going to do about it?" Certainly there were times when issues in manufacturing caused a temporary shortage of supplies; or, parts shipments from overseas were delayed, which caused some backorder situations; or, due to sickness, geography, scheduling, or a perfect storm of service disasters at multiple locations, a technician was not available. However, fortunately for me and my sales team, these occurrences were infrequent. I would say, in the course of all events, these situations occurred in single digit percentages. However, when they did happen, they were very costly to my customers.

Now let's imagine for a moment that the on-time delivery of supplies/parts and service occurred only 47.8% of the time it was promised (Here's the link to our 47.8% forecast accuracy). Again we'll ask, what kind of impact would that have on our customers? What kind of impact would that have on our company? Finally, how long would it take our competition to leverage our miserable performance levels to their advantage? On this last point, I would say just a few nano-seconds.

"OK, so our forecast accuracy is only 47.8% Hey, it's only forecasting. It's always been like this. Companies just deal with it. As a manger, I just pare down my team's forecast and it all works out, right?" Sure companies deal with it. They deal with in ways such as carrying costs for unsold inventories; they deal with it by absorbing exorbitant cost of sales for salaries, travel, and expenses for reps whose forecasts don't materialize. Oh yes, and this one is the most fun to deal with: CEO's deal with board of directors, shareholders, and Wall Street analysts when bogus sales forecasts cause the company to miss revenue projections. "Hey, it's only a few hundred million in market cap, that's all."

A few years ago I was delivering a training session on questioning techniques to about 45 sales reps and managers when the CEO walked in unexpectedly. "Hey

Dean, nice to see you" I said as he sat down in the back of the room. "Hi Dave. I just dropped in for a few moments to see how things are going with the training." I don't know why I did what I did next, but ever since that experience I do the same thing every time an executive joins my class. "Hey Dean, can I ask you a quick question?" "Sure, Dave, go ahead." "Dean, as you look outside the four walls of this building (we were at the corporate headquarters for the training), what are the most pressing challenges the company is currently facing?" Well Dave, clearly we are facing a number of specific challenges from an external perspective. As you know our competition is formidable (the company was competing with Kodak and Xerox on a global level). Secondly, we all are aware of the challenging economic conditions we are currently experiencing that impacts both demand for our product as well as our customer's ability to obtain credit and financing. At the same time, we continue to be challenged by our customers to meet their increasing demand for higher value and quality. And certainly, there is a tremendous amount of pressure on the entire organization to deliver value to our shareholders." "Dean, what specific initiatives has the company adopted in response to these challenges?" "Well Dave, there are a number of specific initiatives. We are automating processes and operations in our manufacturing facilities in order to cut costs and reduce operating expenses. At the same time we continue to invest in new product development. Of course, we are doing everything we can to enable our selling efforts. That's why you're here Dave. To help the folks in this room sell more product so we can make our sales forecast." "I understand and I certainly appreciate your support for this training program. Let me ask you one more question Dean. In looking out over the next 6 to 12 months, what is going to happen if you are not successful in achieving your objectives?" To this point, Dean was very quick to answer every question. His answers were top of mind so to speak. However, when I asked Dean this last question he paused and looked up at the ceiling for a moment to give himself time to think about his answer. "Well Dave, I guess the first thing that will happen is, I'll get fired." Wow! First of all, I had no idea Dean was going to walk into my training session that day. Second, Dean had no idea I was going to ask him any questions at all. Third, in just about 5 minutes, with a few directive and incisive questions, Dean admitted in front of his regional managers and sales team that if the company did not achieve their initiatives, including hitting their forecast, he would be fired. Guess what happened? At the close of that quarter, this company did miss their projections. Wall Street responded with a $250,000,000 drop in market cap. And, Dean's prediction turned into reality; he was fired. "OK, so our forecast accuracy is only 47.8% Hey, it's only forecasting. It's always been like this. Companies just deal with it. Right?" Yes, they do deal with it. Post Script: The incoming CEO's first request was for me to deliver a training session on forecast accuracy at their upcoming sales kick-off meeting.

It Means Our Sales Productivity Stinks! And What You Smell Is the Burning Platform You're Standing On!

Let me repeat my words to the sales professionals from the burning platform chapter. If the CSO Insights numbers we reviewed are not in themselves compelling to you, if as a sales manager these numbers do not make at least some of the hairs on the back of your neck stand up, if you are not choking just a bit from the smoke and flames rising up from the burning platform you're standing on, you are either running a sales organization that is completely anomalous to the 1,500 companies surveyed by CSO Insights, or you are running a sales organization in a territory called the state of denial!

For the rest of us here on planet earth, let's visit the most compelling inspiration I had for writing this book; an event that occurred in the spring of 1979 during an executive meeting in the Schaumburg, IL offices of a little company called Motorola.

"Our Quality Stinks!"

A little background first. On September 25, 1928, in Chicago, IL, Paul V. Galvin and his brother Joseph founded the Galvin Manufacturing Corporation, later renamed Motorola in 1948. Their first product was called a battery eliminator. The device enabled battery-powered radios to run on standard household electric current. In 1958, Motorola introduced the Motrac radio, the world's first vehicular two-way radio. In 1963, Motorola introduced the world's first truly rectangular color TV picture tube. By 1970, Motorola had established itself as the world leader in wireless communication products, while they competed with Texas Instruments and Intel for the top position in semiconductor sales. By 1974, Motorola was one of five American companies leading the world in semiconductor manufacturing with three European companies rounding out the top eight.

However, by 1979, two of these eight manufacturers were Japanese companies. Between 1970 and 1979 the competitive onslaught from Japanese manufacturers cascaded over to consumer products. Quality had become the battleground and Motorola was taking serious casualties. For example, Matsushita was producing TV sets with 7 problems per 100 sets while Motorola was experiencing 140 problems per 100 sets. In other words, Matsushita incidence of defects was just 7%. Conversely, Motorola was producing TV sets with a 140% incidence of defects.

It was May of 1979 when Motorola's Chairman, Robert W. Galvin, 52 years with the company founded by his father and uncle, called a meeting of his executives to address and resolve the growing problem with Japanese competitive dominance. At this point, we will engage in a little creative non-fiction writing and make some assumptions about what was said during this meeting. If our own experience in meetings such as this is any indication, we can assume there was a fair share of finger pointing and passing the blame to someone or something else. However, one individual, Art Sundry, the most senior sales vice-president of the largest communications group at Motorola, is reported to have actually shouted out above the noise that he had something to say that was more important than anything else on the agenda. In quite plain terms, Art verbally challenged the assembly, including Chairman Bob Galvin, when he exclaimed, "Our quality stinks!"

We can only imagine the silence that likely ensued, save the sound of chairs sliding across the floor as those sitting next to Art pulled away to avoid the impending onslaught from the chairman. While we can only speculate on the immediate response, in reality Bob Galvin would later state, "That was a lucky break for us, that we had someone who had the guts to do that and caused all the rest of us who were sitting there to say, 'if Art says that, maybe there's something to it.'" History shows there was infinitely more than just "something to it". In fact, with Art Sundry's wake up call came the birth of the quality transformation at Motorola.

Our Quality Stinks & Here's What We're Going to Do About It.

Bob Galvin began by rolling out Motorola's four-point plan.

1. Global Competitiveness
2. Participative Management
3. Quality Improvements
4. Motorola Training and Education Center

Galvin called for a ten-fold improvement in quality in five years, which was extended to become a hundred-fold improvement in ten years. To support the initiatives, the Motorola Manufacturing Institute was established in 1984, later it was renamed the Motorola Management Institute.

OK, We've Got Great Initiatives.

Has Anyone Figured Out How We're Going to Do It?

Although Galvin had committed the company to a quality improvement transformation, it was clear that Motorola did not have a methodology for a systematic implementation of the improvement initiatives. An interesting side note here is that this realization came almost six years after the May 1979 "Our quality stinks!" proclamation by Art Sundry and ensuing epiphany experienced by Bob Galvin and his executive team. The lesson learned by 1985 was that Bob Galvin's four-point plan, on its own, was not sufficient in terms of accomplishing the company's objectives; shades of Deming's "doing your best is not good enough" edict.

Fortunately, in the fall of 1985, another individual at Motorola was about to make history. Bill Smith, a vice president with Motorola's Land Mobile Products Sector, presented his Six Sigma concept to Bob Galvin. Commonly recognized today as the father of Six Sigma, Bill Smith's Six Sigma approach resulted in Motorola receiving its' first Malcolm Baldrige National Quality Award from the U.S. Government in 1988.

By definition, Bill Smith's Six Sigma methodology was elegantly simple.

Measure process variation and defects

Analyze the data and localize the problem(s)

Improve the process and performance

Control the process

(Later on, **D**efine the Opportunity was added to the initial **MAIC** model to form what is now known as the **DMAIC** model.) Now, please understand that since its origin there have been volumes and volumes written on the 5 steps of the **DMAIC** model. So, for my Six Sigma Green Belt and Black Belt readers, please forgive the simplicity of the representation here as we apply **DMAIC** to the process of selling.

Bill Smith's Six Sigma was embraced at Motorola resulting in the following achievements between 1987 and 1997.

- Five-fold growth in sales, with profits climbing nearly 20 percent per year.

- Cumulative savings based on Six Sigma efforts pegged at 14 billion USD.

- Motorola stock price gains compounded to an annual rate of 21.3 percent.

Bill Smith's Six Sigma had taken root helping to fuel the rapidly growing process improvement revolution in American industry. Among the first to adopt Six Sigma were Allied Signal and General Electric. Regarding the impact of Six Sigma, Jack Welch, former CEO of GE, would later say "I describe Six Sigma as the most important initiative GE has ever undertaken." Today, Six Sigma has been successfully implemented by thousands of companies around the globe. In fact, I would wager that if you work for a large organization you probably know a few Six Sigma Green Belts and/or Black Belts employed at your company by their first names.

Another Great Story.
What Does This Have to Do With Selling?

Boy I'm glad I asked this question. Let's say you work at a company that has adopted Six Sigma process improvement methodologies to the nth degree. While n^{th} is not a Six Sigma measurement, let me explain here what is. Six Sigma is a measure of process capability. A level of Six Sigma means that for every 1 million opportunities there are only 3.4 defects. That means the process is 99.9997% capable of achieving 100% efficiency. Remember that in 1979 Motorola was producing 100 TV sets with 140 defects.

If your company manufactures a product to a level of Six Sigma capability, you have reached a very high degree of quality and efficiency. However, the reason to pursue quality is not for quality's sake alone. To further distill Dr. Deming's views on quality's benefits; quality yields lower costs, more customers, and more jobs. Makes perfect sense doesn't it? What doesn't make sense is the following. Whether your company employs Six Sigma methodologies or not, the chances are they are investing a huge amount of time, money and effort to produce the highest quality product possible to meet their customer's expectations. Here comes the good part. Then, they hand this wonderful high quality product over to the sales team and say: "By the way, we in operations are laboring under Six Sigma standards of 99.9997% efficiency. However, we understand that only 58.8% of your sales organization is meeting performance expectations. We also understand that you are forecasting closed sales at a rate of only 48.7% accuracy. Finally, we know that 20% of your organization is generating a full 62.9% of the revenues of this company while 80% are generating only 37.1%. Hey, that's actually a pretty wide spread in selling efficiency across your organization. Anyway, here's the product, and you guys just do the very best you can, which is not so good by the way, because the truth is, no one else around here understands the sales process so what else can we expect?" Then they walk away and when they get back on the production floor, whisper to each other, "Our sales productivity stinks!"

That's what Six Sigma has to do with selling. Let's get back to step 1 of the 12 steps, acknowledging that we have a chronic and persistent problem that we are incapable of fixing on our own. We must first admit that our sales productivity stinks and things ain't getting any better. The CSO Insights statistics, year after year, are empirical proof that this is true. Second, we must also understand that as Dr. Deming told us, our good intentions and doing our best is just not good enough. We have to know what to do and then do our best. It is clear that despite the ongoing investment in sales training, despite all the best practices we are not sharing across the organization, despite the must have CRM implementations that are ineffective at best, we really don't know how to fix the problem.

Two 'You Cannot...' Truths

You can conduct all the lifeboat drills you want and fire all the underperforming reps every 6 to 12 months. However, there are two truths you must understand at this point.

You Cannot Hire Enough Capable Individuals to Reverse The 80/20 Rule.

20% of the sales reps are generating 61.5% of revenues while 80% are generating just 38.5% of revenues. Regardless of all of the programs for hiring the right kind of talent, which are worth their weight in gold if they were actually used, the statistics show that over 50% of companies are not applying skills assessments as part of the hiring criteria. The reality is, if it were possible to hire enough capable individuals, you would have already done so.

You Cannot Train Enough Capable Individuals to Build A Capable Sales Organization.

The performance statistics from CSO Insights just do not support this as a viable strategy. Despite the fact that the average company invests approx. $1,500 per year per sales rep, sales productivity continues to be mired at sub-performance levels that are not meeting expectations.

"Hold on a second Dave. We've got that fire, hire and train strategy cooking for us. What's wrong with that? And besides, aren't you in the business of sales training? Are you saying sales training doesn't work?"

I can't take credit for being the first one to say it, but yes, that's exactly what I'm saying!

Chapter 2

Sales Training Doesn't Work!

A few years back, I was co-delivering a 3-day sales training class at a learning campus in a beautiful little town called Feldafing located on the west shore of Lake Starnberg, southwest of Munich, Germany. We had a great session, and it was time for my colleague to wrap things up with the group of 30 or so sales managers. My co-facilitator, who I will simply call 'D', is in my view a world-class facilitator, elite sales professional, and above all, through-and-through, a Brit from the U.K. In other words, using the vernacular, he has a 'fantastic' sense of the driest humor and wit, which he masterfully doles out at just the right moments during training sessions. It's simply brilliant! Of course, the art in his delivery is the audience rarely sees it coming. At the end of this particular session which had been very well received by the participants, 'D' stood up to address the group. In a very serious manner, D talked about how the value of what we had learned can only be measured by how well we apply the learning in our everyday sales lives once we return to our respective countries, regions, districts and territories. In this weighty context, 'D' then made the following proclamation, in a somewhat challenging fashion. "Therefore, I must tell you that sales training doesn't work!" He then paused, as all skilled orators do, to observe the response from his audience. You can just imagine the looks of horror! The gasps of disbelief! The uneasy shifting in chairs. The leaning over to adjacent colleagues whispering, "He didn't just say that out loud, did he?" Did our fantastic facilitator and esteemed instructor just tell us that our three days of suffering and 'learning through the struggle', not to mention the sleep deprivation from late sessions at dinner followed by the requisite rounds of libations at the bar, were all in vain? "Oh the humanity!" Then, just before the weeping and wailing, and gnashing of the teeth exceeded what could be humanly endured, and literally seconds before business casual apparel was rent in two, 'D' snatched the crowd from complete despair and said, "…Unless of course, you do something with it."

Step back from the precipice! Come down off the ledge! Of course sales training doesn't work unless we do something with it. Of course, everyone knows that! We are saved after all! When large groups of individuals travel across the globe; when the company and staff invest precious time out of the field; when we completely empty our heads of all distractions and internalize every golden nugget possible from impeccable content delivered in three days of drinking from a fire hose; of course we know that the ultimate success of this colossal investment hinges entirely on each individuals commitment to actually applying the 'learnings' in the field. Of course! Isn't that why 'D' was being so artfully facetious in his classic British style? And because we all know this; isn't it exactly why sales training does work?

'D' and I actually have a few colleagues who don't quite appreciate the little 'gotcha' he employs to wrap up his sessions. Why? The truth of the matter is this; they don't like it because 'D' is right! Here's another reason they don't appreciate it. Because they're convicted! They know that most sales training is ineffective; they are in denial about it; they don't want to be associated with failure; and, they think that if we don't overtly state it, the participants in their training sessions are too naive to figure it out. Note to facilitators: They know! Instead of at least being honest about it, these folks would rather engage in a group high five on the limo ride back to the airport while taking turns recounting how great their delivery was. "Yea, I know, I was there, remember?"

Now wait a minute Dave; aren't you being a little tough on your fellow facilitators? My guess is only they, along with the learning & development staff who hire and work with them, would think so. The perception from the sales side of the house is more likely in line with my comments. However, don't take my word for it. Let's take a look at how some of the experts see it.

Measuring the Effectiveness of Training

Donald Kirkpatrick, PhD, Professor Emeritus, University of Wisconsin, introduced his 4-step model for evaluating training effectiveness in 1959; his book, *Evaluating Training Programs* was published in 1975. Today, Professor Kilpatrick's model is arguably the most widely accepted methodology in use for evaluating training and learning programs.

Kirkpatrick Model for Evaluating Effectiveness of Training Programs

Level 4 - Results	**What organizational benefits resulted from the training?**
Level 3 - Behavior	**To what extent did participants change their behavior back in the workplace, as a result of the training?**
Level 2 - Learning	**To what extent did participants improve knowledge and skills and change attitudes, as a result of the training?**
Level 1 - Reaction	**How did participants react to the program?**

Level 1 – Reaction. Most programs that I have been involved with for Fortune 500 companies have an evaluation form filled out by the participants at the end of the class. There are a number of categories for evaluation ranging from: pre-class instructions; to competence of the facilitator; to applicability of the content; to conduciveness of the facilities for learning. Generally, the threshold for acceptable performance across all metrics is a 4.0 out of 5.0 rating or 80%. When a rating is lower than 4.0, changes are made to the program. I think Level 1 – Reaction is handled very well by most learning & development organizations.

Level 2 – Learning. Here again, we will refer back to the course evaluation with specific ratings for knowledge and skills improvement. In my experience, most participants agree their knowledge improved as a result of sales training. Skills on the other hand are more difficult to improve within the short time period of a training session. Most participants agree that with practice, their skills will likely improve in the future. Here is where we begin to detect some pin holes in the dike. Of course skills improve with practice. However, once they leave the forced practice environment of the classroom, with exercises and role-plays, will they practice in the field on their own? More on this later.

Level 3 – Behavior. To what extent did participants change their behavior back in the workplace as a result of the training? Now here's where we need to enlist much more than a little Dutch boy to stick his finger in the dike. There are two great joys for those of us who facilitate. The first is the 'ah-ha!' moment when the light of understanding turns on for a participant after the initial period of confusion or perhaps denial. It's when something just 'clicks', and suddenly they get it. The ah-ha moment is one of the things we facilitators strive to achieve in the classroom. Unfortunately, we never experience the mass hysteria phenomenon where one individual gets it, and all of a sudden, we have the entire classroom falling down prostrate row after row or table after table. A modest amount of ah-ha's means you've had a good class. The second great joy of facilitating, that happens all too seldom, is the testimonial e-mail. The following is an example of one of these e-mails sent to me by a former student.

> Hello Dave,
>
> I wanted to tell you about two recent accounts that resulted in sales. I used what the course in Atlanta showed me to prepare. I was attempting to close the old way by going in and just pushing for the close. After your course I did the 1st email to ABC Co. using the method you taught us; success! Then I did the same with XYZ Corp., success again!
> Thanks for all your help,
>
> Michael

I have taught thousands of sales professionals all over the globe, and I only wish I had thousands of testimonials to show for it. In fact, here is a more accurate account of what is retained after participants leave the classroom. Recently I conducted a quick two-hour session on the West Coast for a group of sales managers. The content of the session was actually a shortened version of a full one-day session I had delivered several times previously to the same business unit. In the class of 50 managers, there were three that had been in one of these previous sessions. We discovered this after the sideways glances and exchanges of, "Say, I was in one of your classes before. Now which one was it? Oh yes, that's it." Of course my response was, "OK, we have three experts with us who have gone through the one day session who can now come up to the front of the room and teach today." The immediate reply from my three alumni was not so flattering in terms of the impact the previous class had on them. "Now wait a minute! That was a year ago. I don't remember enough to even comment about the class let alone teach it." While we all had a good laugh, the reality of the comment is not laughable at all. I think if we are honest and charted the Kilpatrick model we would start to see something like this.

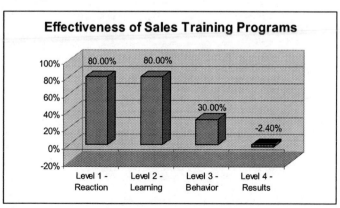

141

We'll give Level 1 and Level 2 an 80% since that is the learning & development minimum requirement for successful delivery of the content. However, for Level 3, actual changes in behavior, I would estimate it at about 30%. Why just 30%? Here's another example.

Earlier this year I was delivering a session in North Carolina. The company does a neat thing at the end of the first day of the three day session. A visiting executive comes in and spends an hour in Q&A with the class. In this particular session, one of the participants asked the visiting Senior VP if the company was making an attempt to train the managers so that the content would have some reinforcement, continuity, and sponsorship in the field. Otherwise, the participant commented, the learning will be lost. Sound familiar? By the way, I get this question from participants in just about every session where managers are not required to attend the class. The executive answered with the following. "I understand your concern, and I know that probably 70% of the people who attend classes don't apply the learning for various reasons…" I was shocked and not surprised at the same time. Shocked that this executive of a multi-billion dollar organization would admit, accept and therefore play a role in perpetuating this dismal rate of adoption while his company invested millions of dollars per year in training. In fact, he made these comments as we all sat in an absolutely beautiful corporate university facility; no small investment there either. At the same time I was completely not surprised by the fact that in his view 70% of the participants don't apply the learning. Why? Because I agreed with him. Sales training doesn't work, remember?

Finally we come to Level 4 – Results. Again, we need only look as far as the findings from CSO Insights 2009 report for objective empirical data. I'll just repeat a few of the most telling statistics from the previous chapter with emphasis on the final bullet point.

- Approx. **50%** of companies invest an average of **$1,500** in sales training annually per sales rep.

- Regarding training in the areas of sales skills, sales process, the marketplace, justifying the purchase, sales management, and CRM application, approx. **50%** of companies said that the training was not meeting expectations.

- **58.8%** of sales reps are meeting or exceeding quota. This number is down from **61.2%** in 2008.

- **20%** of the sales reps are generating **61.5%** of revenues. **80%** are generating just **38.5%** of revenues.

- Only **47.8%** of forecasted deals are won. **30.4%** are lost deals and **21.9%** result in no decision.

- Only **30%** of companies consistently use the sales methodology taught in sales training.

The net result is sales performance in 2009 is down 2.4% from 2008 figures. Would you say that more than 30% of your reps consistently apply what they learn in sales training sessions? If so, I invite you to contact me and share your secrets of adoption success.

Let's do a little math and dig a little deeper into the CSO numbers. You tell me if the following analysis is in error. The average company is investing $1,500 in sales training per rep per year. This typical company also has a sales rep turnover of 28.4%; voluntary (rep leaves) of 15.3%; involuntary (rep is let go) of 13.1%. That means that 28.4% of the sales reps are receiving new hire training. The remaining 71.6% of the incumbent sales reps are therefore receiving additional training on top of the training done in previous years. Assuming we have ramp up time, we can deduce that although 71.6% of the sales force, the incumbents, have been the beneficiaries of additional training, the results show that the number of reps meeting or exceeding quota actually declined from 61.2% in 2008 to 58.8% in 2009. Again, that is a decrease in performance of 2.4%.

These statistics raise some interesting questions. Can we make an argument that the $1,500 investment per sales rep is actually contributing to decreased performance levels? Or, since only 30% of folks actually apply what they have learned does it mean that the problem is not content but rather adoption and compliance? If that is true, could it be that the 30% of reps who applied what they learned actually sold more, while the 70% who do not apply the learning performed so poorly they dragged down the rest of the team with them? You know what? It is very unlikely we can answer any of these questions because the data we need to determine what is really contributing to poor performance is not available to us. Why? It's not in our CRM!

A recent Butler Group report found that 70% of CRM implementations fail. A Gartner study found that approximately 55% of all CRM projects failed to meet customers' expectations. While there are a multitude of reasons cited for failure of CRM projects, user acceptance is the one of the most critical factors. In other words, because of lack of acceptance and compliance, the data is just not there.

Let's take another look at our Kilpatrick chart.

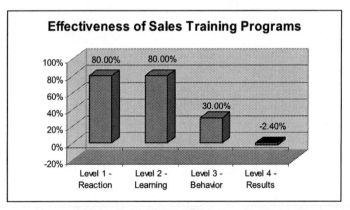

At least 80% of sales reps participating in sales training react positively to the content and admit they are learning something. However, when they get back in the field, only 30% are applying what they have learned resulting in an actual decrease in sales productivity in 2009 of 2.4%. Say it with me: "Oh the humanity!"

Is sales training working in your organization? Care to take a little test? The following is a list of 50 observations by Dr. John Sullivan, Head, and Professor, of Human Resource Management College of Business, San Francisco State University. By the way, Professor Sullivan takes a similar view on training to my friend 'D'. Indicate your agreement, or disagreement, to each point on a scale of 1 – Disagree, to 5 - Agree, on the right of each of Dr. Sullivan's observations. Then average the total at the end. If your average is closer to 5 than 1, then you agree that training in your organization is largely ineffective.

Professor Sullivan:
A Great Deal of Corporate Training Is Irrelevant.
What Is Wrong With Most Corporate Training:

Regarding Training:

1	Most training functions are independent. They are often removed from HR, knowledge management, competitive intelligence, educational assistance (degree programs), OD, OE and benchmarking activities. The silo approach keeps solutions from being integrated into the strategic business plan.	1 2 3 4 5 ⭘⭘⭘ ⭘⭘ Disagree Agree
2	Few training departments even have a name for their strategy. Those that do often use terms like "developing a learning organization," but few managers or trainers can define what that really means.	1 2 3 4 5 ⭘⭘⭘ ⭘⭘ Disagree Agree

3	The image of training is often poor. Politically training is often weak, and it ends up being the first program that is cut in tough times, because they haven't sold the CEO/ CFO on their value. Training needs to develop its own brand and image both inside and outside the firm. Training needs to be a key tool in attracting (employer of choice), and retaining the very best.	1 2 3 4 5 ○ ○ ○ ○ ○ Disagree Agree
4	Most training designs were developed from the education model. New models (e-commerce, mass customization, JIT, distance learning and self-service) need to be added to the mix of strategies.	1 2 3 4 5 ○ ○ ○ ○ ○ Disagree Agree
5	Almost all training programs are pre-event based. Almost none are current problem based. Training needs to design on-line systems that walk a manager through each of the steps that a manager needs to follow in order to solve their day to day problems. Training departments need to work with HR to develop 'expert systems' to guide managers through their day-to-day events like discipline, sexual harassment, retention etc.	1 2 3 4 5 ○ ○ ○ ○ ○ Disagree Agree
6	Most training programs are developed over a period of months, while management problems occur overnight. Program development must include just-in-time capabilities. Training must be JIT if it is to add real value in a rapidly changing world. If you can't develop and apply it right away, then forget it.	1 2 3 4 5 ○ ○ ○ ○ ○ Disagree Agree
7	Most training 'needs assessments' are historical and backward focused. Training needs to fore-cast and anticipate problems as well. It needs smoke detectors to let managers know they have potential problems that are training related before they get out of hand. It should also have SWAT type teams to rapidly address crisis training needs.	1 2 3 4 5 ○ ○ ○ ○ ○ Disagree Agree

8	A great deal of training is done by outside vendors. We can't beat out competitors if they can buy the same training we can.	1 2 3 4 5 ○ ○ ○ ○ ○ Disagree Agree
9	Training is done too far in advance of the perceived need, and, as a result, attendees often fail to pay sufficient attention. Do just-before-the-need training so that participants can see the direct/immediate relevance of the training. In a fast changing world, training that doesn't use the latest technology and that isn't continually updated has no value. Just-in-time training program development allows managers to use training as an answer to spot or address emergency problems.	1 2 3 4 5 ○ ○ ○ ○ ○ Disagree Agree
10	Training programs need to learn from their successes and failures. There needs to be a feedback loop between performance data, performance appraisals, pay increases etc. so that programs can improve based on how they do, or don't, impact actual performance.	1 2 3 4 5 ○ ○ ○ ○ ○ Disagree Agree
11	Training on the run, offered a minute here and there (even an audiotape to listen during the commute might work better), is one new model that needs to be adopted because workloads are so demanding, as a result of downsizing and growth. Remote, distance, and self-paced self-service learning need to become the norm rather than the exception.	1 2 3 4 5 ○ ○ ○ ○ ○ Disagree Agree
12	Most training targets low performers but not the high performers that make us most of our profit. By dumbing training down to fit the masses, training loses all value to high performers. Training refuses to treat top performers differently. An overemphasis on equality is a mistake.	1 2 3 4 5 ○ ○ ○ ○ ○ Disagree Agree

13	Most training is non-competitive. Few training departments do a program-by-program competitive analysis (like product units do), so they cannot tell if our training gives our firm a competitive advantage! Others buy off the shelf materials that competitors can also buy. Canned material isn't likely to fit your unique needs either.	1 2 3 4 5 ○ ○ ○ ○ ○ Disagree Agree
14	Most training doesn't work, because research studies show 70% or more of all learning occurs outside the classroom. Trainers need to identify where learning occurs and 'go there'.	1 2 3 4 5 ○ ○ ○ ○ ○ Disagree Agree
15	Training functions fail to ask the best performers, experts, how they learn. By finding out how the best get so smart, you can learn about new and other methods that work in the real world.	1 2 3 4 5 ○ ○ ○ ○ ○ Disagree Agree
16	Executives often need different types of training than most managers. Different strategies and tools need to be developed for different targeted groups. Training budgets and programs need to be prioritized to the business needs. Equity needs to be replaced with programs that are unequal so that key programs and top performers get a disproportionate amount of training attention.	1 2 3 4 5 ○ ○ ○ ○ ○ Disagree Agree
17	Training needs to tie its databases to internal business databases (sales, customer service ratings, market share, turnover rates, employee surveys, 360 degree assessments and market research), as well as to external databases (Unemployment, economic growth, competitive analysis, university graduation rates etc.), in order to improve training, and to anticipate such things as the quality and availability of new hires, business growth, etc.	1 2 3 4 5 ○ ○ ○ ○ ○ Disagree Agree

18	Training is a very conservative function. It teaches the basics but seldom offers leading edge learning (which top performers, design and IT professionals demand). It often has a social work mentality that encourages it to offer all programs to all people.	1 2 3 4 5 ○ ○ ○ ○ ○ Disagree Agree
19	Training needs to become more experimental and scientific. It needs to try more pilot programs, as well as applying split sample programs, so that the results in a control department can be compared to the results of the experimental group.	1 2 3 4 5 ○ ○ ○ ○ ○ Disagree Agree
20	Most employee training is independent of customer and sales training. This independence allows for disconnects between these vital strategic components. Integration would speed up shared learning.	1 2 3 4 5 ○ ○ ○ ○ ○ Disagree Agree
21	Most training programs are broad based but individuals have specific training and growth expectations. Training needs to help managers develop individual growth and learning plans for all key employees. Lack of training, challenge, and growth are key factors that cause top performing employees to leave.	1 2 3 4 5 ○ ○ ○ ○ ○ Disagree Agree

Regarding Training Design:

22	Some employees are self-developers and don't need formal training. They resent being sent and wonder why weak employees can afford to be away from work learning things that self-developing workers learn on their own.	1 2 3 4 5 ○ ○ ○ ○ ○ Disagree Agree
23	All employees don't learn at the same speed. Provide self-directed, self-service learning so employees can move at their own speed. Training can't be offered in a one size fits all approach. It is seldom tailored to different learning styles or speeds. Global firms require mass customized solutions. Offering multiple options (self-service, individual attention, a choice of mediums, lengths etc.) and identifying everyone's learning preferences and what actually works for them is required.	1 2 3 4 5 ○ ○ ○ ○ ○ Disagree Agree
24	Training often piles on information, hoping some of it will be relevant. Trainees can't be over-loaded with information; instead, they need to get targeted information in just the right amount that they need.	1 2 3 4 5 ○ ○ ○ ○ ○ Disagree Agree
25	Whenever possible, work with recruitment to hire individuals who are continuous learning, self-developing individuals, so that you can do less formal training.	1 2 3 4 5 ○ ○ ○ ○ ○ Disagree Agree
26	A good deal of training is designed for individ-uals, while most work is done in teams. Provide team based on-the-job training for workgroups.	1 2 3 4 5 ○ ○ ○ ○ ○ Disagree Agree
27	Trainers want you to come during business hours and to their site. Trainers need to come to the site during times convenient for the trainee.	1 2 3 4 5 ○ ○ ○ ○ ○ Disagree Agree

28	Training programs generally come in large chunks which can overwhelm managers and employees. Training needs to be delivered in just the amount the person needs. Training should be able to mass customize it's product into separable modules and pieces. If it is not, people can be overwhelmed, and, as a result, they tend to postpone training until they have time or when it is too late. All training seems to be designed in 2 hour, half and whole-day increments. Some learning only takes minutes.	1 2 3 4 5 ○ ○ ○ ○ ○ Disagree Agree
29	Most training is static. Knowledge needs to be moved rapidly around an organization, if it is to be used to solve problems. Sharing what works needs to be rapid and automatic, not just boxed into a class.	1 2 3 4 5 ○ ○ ○ ○ ○ Disagree Agree
30	Training often follows a one-time deliver and forget approach. Without on-the-job follow up and coaching, it is likely to fail. Learning is a continuous and ongoing process.	1 2 3 4 5 ○ ○ ○ ○ ○ Disagree Agree
31	It requires too much off-the-job time. In a world with heavy performance incentives, people want their training to have a higher ROI than if they stayed on-the-job. It seldom does. It has little data to prove that it really does change behavior or improve performance. Trainers need to provide data on the knowledge, behavior, and performance change that an attendee can expect from each class.	1 2 3 4 5 ○ ○ ○ ○ ○ Disagree Agree
32	Most training departments lack a strategic vision. Trainers need to integrate classes and show how this micro training topic fits into the firm's big picture.	1 2 3 4 5 ○ ○ ○ ○ ○ Disagree Agree

33	Other non-training options need to be included in the mix. Consider providing copies of article and book summaries as short, quick learning tools. Put the training on a CD, or Intranet, so they can access it anytime. Add non-traditional (non-classroom) training as an alternate approach to learning. Some suggestions include the distribution of best practices manuals, watch while you are at home videos, electronic bulletin boards, on-line chat groups, and professional conferences as alternative.	1 2 3 4 5 ○ ○ ○ ○ ○ Disagree Agree
34	Training is often used as a tool to postpone decisions on poor performers. It's easy to send them to more training, but it just postpones the inevitable. Some individuals learn on their own, while others are rewarded with time off from work to attend training sessions.	1 2 3 4 5 ○ ○ ○ ○ ○ Disagree Agree
35	Most don't voluntarily go to training. If it is required, there is automatic resistance. Survey those who do not attend to find out why (they are voting with their feet against what you are doing).	1 2 3 4 5 ○ ○ ○ ○ ○ Disagree Agree
36	Most training is designed for the U.S. culture. In a global market, training must be customized to fit diverse cultures and be available in multiple languages 24 hours a day.	1 2 3 4 5 ○ ○ ○ ○ ○ Disagree Agree
37	Training uses its own language. Many trainers speak "psycho-babble" and don't ever use business terms like ROI, profit, and competitive advantage. Often degrees in education and psychology give them little credibility in a world dominated by engineering and business degrees. Most trainers have never rotated into line jobs, so they are disconnected from the business. It has jargon and fads that confuse most workers. Training needs to use the language of business and avoid fads that lessen its credibility.	1 2 3 4 5 ○ ○ ○ ○ ○ Disagree Agree

38	In addition to traditional paper documents and lecture formats, managers and employees need to be able to do what-if and if-then scenarios (on-line), to prepare them for future problems and opportunities.	1 2 3 4 5 O O O O O Disagree Agree
39	Training is almost always isolated from educational assistance programs. The programs need to be coordinated, and their ROI's need to be compared.	1 2 3 4 5 O O O O O Disagree Agree
40	Person-to-person learning tools, such as mentors, part-time job rotations, apprentice programs, internal/ external expert lists, are often underutilized.	1 2 3 4 5 O O O O O Disagree Agree

Regarding Training Delivery:

41	Training isn't delivered by successful managers with credibility. Most trainers are not subject matter experts. As a result, their knowledge is often shallow. No matter how technically good they are, life long trainers need to rotate into real jobs frequently in order to build their credibility and knowledge.	1 2 3 4 5 O O O O O Disagree Agree
42	Managers don't own most training. Get managers who are well respected to sponsor the training session. Let the managers help design it, or let the star performers (employees) present it. Get the CEO to attend. Let your customers do some of the presentations.	1 2 3 4 5 O O O O O Disagree Agree
43	Most training does not involve the audience in their own learning. They can sit on their hands and listen. Stop lecturing...do action learning. Learning only sticks when you can feel it and touch it.	1 2 3 4 5 O O O O O Disagree Agree

44	GenXer's (and others) have short attention spans while trainers only work in one-hour intervals. Shorten the training sessions to 15-30 minutes to keep up the interest of those with short attention spans.	1 2 3 4 5 ○ ○ ○ ○ ○ Disagree Agree
45	Most of the topics taught in training are flavor-of-the-month fads that have no lasting value.	1 2 3 4 5 ○ ○ ○ ○ ○ Disagree Agree
46	Most training teaches facts but not how to think and learn. Knowledge changes rapidly, so the useful life of training knowledge is limited. If attendees aren't excited about learning, it will be a one-time event. Benchmarking often provides more credible information faster and cheaper.	1 2 3 4 5 ○ ○ ○ ○ ○ Disagree Agree
47	Workers don't have time for classroom training that requires on-site attendance. Travel expenses and time away from the job combined make it too expensive for remote workers to attend.	1 2 3 4 5 ○ ○ ○ ○ ○ Disagree Agree
48	Most training isn't fun. Instead, it's too long, it's provided in a one-way communication format, and it assumes all knowledge comes from the teacher, as opposed to also coming from the students. Participants need to be given time to share their problems and solutions among each other.	1 2 3 4 5 ○ ○ ○ ○ ○ Disagree Agree
49	Most employees don't do their pre-work prior to training. As a result, the difference in learning speed between the prepared and the less prepared slows down overall learning and frustrates the ones that did their pre-work.	1 2 3 4 5 ○ ○ ○ ○ ○ Disagree Agree
50	Un-prepared people should not be allowed to attend formalized training sessions.	1 2 3 4 5 ○ ○ ○ ○ ○ Disagree Agree

OK, Where's the Disconnect?

"Sales training doesn't work…unless we do something with it." My friend 'D' knows this to be true, and frankly so does everyone in sales management and learning & development, along with every participant in every sales training class ever delivered. The performance numbers are irrefutable. We are realizing only incremental results for incredible investments in training dollars. The Kilpatrick training effectiveness model tells us the disconnect occurs almost immediately after participants leave the classroom.

Why are 'D' and I, and other sales facilitators, resorting to begging, pleading, cajoling participants into actually using what they have learned when they get out in the field? Why do we have to sell sales training?

Sales training is in many cases mandatory. However, mandatory or elective, actually utilizing methodologies taught in the classroom is almost completely elective on the part of the participants. Once they leave the classroom, sales reps are often left to their own devices. Now, does that mean they are not well intended? Of course not! However, good intentions are just that; good intentions. Clearly, we are all well intended. However, the problem with good intentions is this. Because everyone means well the responsibility for failure is more difficult to assess. Is it the training? Is it the content? Is it the facilitator? Is it learning & development?

Is it sales management? Or is it the sales reps themselves? Is it us, or is it them?

I believe Dr. Deming said it almost perfectly when he stated "Failures are the result of systemic problems, not individual shortcomings." When I say Deming's statement is almost perfect what I mean is, unlike manufacturing, which is what Deming primarily focused on, sales is not conducted in a controlled environment. Manufacturing generally occurs on a production floor and therefore, for the most part, it operates in a controlled environment. If something is going wrong, you can simply go out to the production floor and look and see where the defects are occurring. The cause and source of the defects may not be apparent of course, which is the reason for applying Six Sigma methodologies. Deming is saying that when the processes and the systems are efficient, the impact of the individual is minimized. Of course minimizing the individual in the production process also has other trade-offs. Do we need real people or just a bunch of robots? While automation may be good for business it may not be so good for the people who were once employed at the factory.

Like manufacturing, selling is a process. However, selling is not a production line. In sales the contribution and impact of the individual is much greater than it is in a manufacturing environment. Therefore, we cannot dismiss what Dow Chemical calls in their current advertising campaign, 'the human element' from the equation. That also means we cannot relieve the human element from accountability in their role in the process. Distill it all down and what I am saying is failures are in large part the result of systematic problems. However, there is such a thing as a bad hire, or in the words of *Good to Great* author Jim Collins, an individual who does not belong on the bus.

Having said this, here are a few questions for us managers. Can we, and do we, blame sales reps for poor performance when they appeared to be capable and on-fire when we hired them, but then fizzled out in the field? Should we be blaming ourselves as managers for not enforcing the methodologies? And let's not leave out the technology. What about our almighty CRM? Does our CRM implementation facilitate execution in the field? What percentage of your reps regularly use their CRM and when they do, how accurate is the data? In this case I would have to agree with Dr. Deming. The disconnect is not individual shortcomings. The disconnect is in a system that allows individuals to be left to their own good intentions and their own devices. "I use our CRM for some things. I just don't see it helping me achieve my sales targets." So how do we fix the problem? I'm saving that for the chapter on solutions. For now, we're going to spend a bit more time on the burning platform!

It's a Great Day for an Epiphany

In many of the classes I facilitate, right out of the gate, I am faced with a huge potential challenge. Believe it or not, some participants – no one reading this book of course – go into sales training sessions asking themselves: "Why am I here? Clearly there is nothing more I can learn since I have been through it all already." That's why most sales training courses are designed to kick-off with the proverbial 'burning platform'. This is the part where the facilitator challenges your understanding of what you already know and attempts to create a burning platform of urgency under your cushy padded seat in the classroom by making you realize that what you don't know is really killing you. Usually the path to the 'ah-ha', or epiphany, requires the enlistment of a few embarrassed individuals we facilitators must sacrifice at the altar of ignorance-is-bliss. Of course, we do it in the spirit of a safe environment where we are not sacrificing; we are simply challenging and coaching for the benefit of all. I have actually had notes passed to me by learning & development staff at the beginning of a training session identifying the 'wise-guys' in the group who were to be offered up to suffer the flames of the burning platform. At any rate, the CSO findings at the beginning of the Manger's Corner served as the burning platform for you, my manager friends. My sense is you may smell a little smoke and sense some heat, but we still have some way to go. That's ok. I've got plenty of charcoal, lighter fluid, matches, a giant kettle filled with boiling water, a grass skirt and a big spoon. Let's keep going and move on to the dreaded CRM implementation!

Manager's Corner

Chapter 3

"Our CRM Implementation Is Ineffective!"

Sales People Fail Businesses, not CRM Systems

Microsoft Dynamics research reveals that 60% of Sales Directors see CRM as fundamental to their sales process, yet a quarter have lost customers directly because of ineffective use of CRM technology.

Reading, UK – 27 June 2006 - Research commissioned by Microsoft Dynamics shows that one in six sales directors see customer relationship management technology as fundamental to their sales process. However, the ineffective use of CRM is costing many companies dearly.

The research, which surveys 100 sales directors in companies with between 100 and 1000 employees, finds that 56% of respondents do not use their CRM system for sales forecasting – a key strategic benefit of CRM. This may be because many sales teams are not using CRM properly, and, as the survey shows, 44% of sales directors say that fewer that 80% of their sales staff are using CRM effectively. In turn, sales directors are doing little to turn the tide: 72% of sales directors tolerate inefficient use of CRM to some extent within their companies and nearly three-quarters (73%) do not discipline sales staff for their failure to use CRM properly.

Inefficient use of CRM is having a severe knock-on impact on respondents' businesses. Nearly one-quarter (24%) of UK medium-sized businesses have directly lost customers; 48% say they are missing out on potential revenue, and one-third have experienced increased levels of customer dissatisfaction due to poor CRM use.

The key barriers of effective CRM use are that sales people don't like to change the way they work (49% of respondents), and they are resistant to new, and unfamiliar, technologies (37%). If sales directors are to get full benefits from CRM, they should therefore consider implementing easy to use, and familiar, systems to encourage better utilization. If they don't facilitate, or force, their sales people to use CRM properly, sales directors in UK companies ultimately risk losing further potential revenue and more customers as a result.

Is there anything else that needs to be said about, or added to, the Microsoft research? Clearly, this could be the shortest chapter in this book. By the way, I have absolutely no qualms about citing research that is at least three years old, because I know from first hand experience there has been no significant change in these sobering figures. Ineffective use of CRM technology continues to be a world-wide epidemic and chronic problem. Having said there is nothing more to say, let me throw in an additional two-cents worth on the subject.

As a National Sales Manager back in 2002, I conducted my own CRM effectiveness survey of our entire sales force for our business unit. At the time, we had about 85 sales reps in the field, and we were using the top CRM implementation available (I'm sure you can guess which one). Our implementation operated in both on-line and off-line mode. Meaning, we required regular 'syncing' from field reps to ensure that management had an up to date and current view of the CRM data relating to each selling opportunity. My survey showed that compliance, regular syncing, was occurring only about 30% of the time. Therefore, 70% of the data management was viewing was outdated by as much as two weeks. Secondly, the data sales reps were reporting, when they reported, relating to working opportunities (active accounts in the sales funnel), was only about 25% accurate. For example: inaccurate indication of step-of-sale position, erroneous pricing, wrongly projected close dates, and probability to close. Essentially, we had only 30% of the sales reps reporting in a timely manner and overall only 25% accuracy in the data we were looking at. That equates to an efficiency of only 7.5%! Here's the real killer. The company I worked for had invested a minimum of $5,000 per seat, with 16,000 to 24,000 seats. That's an initial investment of $80M to $120M!

In early 2007 I facilitated a class on change management. The audience included the North American Director of Sales for a multi-billion dollar business unit along with about 25 individuals from his sales management team. When I asked about the most pressing current issues they were struggling with relating to change, I thought I would hear about the latest company re-organization or perhaps a revised compensation plan. Instead, what I heard was not a current issue at all. The resounding issues were CRM compliance, shape of the pipeline, and forecast accuracy. All issues they had been struggling with for many years. At one point the Director stood up and chided his managers with the following: "People! Let me be clear. I simply can not run this business with erroneous pipelines and inaccurate forecasting in CRM!" Again, I really see no relative change, in just about every venue. Today, when I facilitate sales training classes, and I mention CRM efficiency, almost without exception, I here snickers, if not outright laughter, from the group.

I find the entire CRM issue absolutely fascinating. CSO Insights reports that 41% of the firms that did not have CRM implemented in 2008 planned to do so in 2009. Adding technology to track sales opportunities through the sales process is obviously, and intuitively, a no-brainer! Who wouldn't want to do that? However, the CSO Insights reveals a shocking reality.

- There does not appear to be any significant singular benefit from reps simply using CRM alone. In fact, the percentage of reps making quota for firms that had CRM system adoption rates of more than 75% of the time was only 59%.

- For inconsistent/infrequent users, clocking in at less than 25% of the time, the percentage of reps making quota was 61%.

- These numbers are hardly a ringing endorsement to get with the program.

- The numbers continue to support what has been repeated over and over about CRM: first get your process straight, *then* automate. That is, technology, in and of itself, is not the silver bullet once hoped for; simply bringing technology into your organization is unlikely to make a major difference – *even with high levels of compliance and use.*

Let's make sure we understand this. Reps with high CRM compliance rates, of greater than 75%, are meeting, or exceeding, quota 59% of the time. Meanwhile, reps with CRM compliance rates of less than 25% are meeting or exceeding quota 61% of the time. I believe there are two explanations for the disparity in these numbers. First, it is an indication that CRM is not being used as an effective strategic tool for driving sales performance. In reality, the majority of companies use CRM as a forensic tool to conduct post mortem's on past events in the sales process. "Hey, I see you didn't make enough face-to-face sales calls last month. Better start making some more calls." "I'm looking at my team's forecasted deals for last quarter and only 48% of them actually closed. We better do some training on closing techniques." Guess what? Post mortem is too late! We're largely using our CRM tool to perform autopsies on dead deals.

The second explanation for the disparity is another all too common practice in the management approach of most sales organizations. When a rep is selling, meaning they are above quota, we don't hassle them with bothersome administrative tasks like doing their CRM. Remember the statistic we cited in the Burning Platform chapter from Microsoft Business Solutions regarding poor CRM compliance? *Sales directors themselves are hardly blameless with 72% confessing that they tolerate inefficient use of the CRM they have invested in.* In other words, managers tend not to force compliance with the 58.8% of their reps who are meeting or exceeding quota. Enter once again the insidiousness of this type of approach. It is difficult, if not impossible, to apply one set of lax standards of CRM compliance for the half of your team that is performing, and another set of strict standards of CRM compliance for the other half of your team that is not performing. It just isn't a practical or natural way to manage.

It is really no wonder CSO Insights says: "these numbers are hardly a ringing endorsement to get with the (CRM) program." Further, is it that difficult to understand why a recent Butler Group report found that 70% of CRM implementations fail? Say what you will, and there is a lot to say about CRM effectiveness, you have to take your hats off to the developers of CRM technology.

It all started back in the mid 80's with Ken Morris and Dave Duffield, founders of PeopleSoft. CRM was originally a human resource based application that began to branch out in the 90's and now supports everything from customer service to supply chains. Then there's Tom Siebel. Siebel was with Oracle in the 80's where he developed a nifty application for internally managing sales accounts. Larry Ellison, Oracle's CEO, refused to fund the project commercially. Siebel then left Oracle and eventually founded Siebel Systems in 1993 along with Patricia House, an Oracle marketing executive. The rest is history as they say, and there's where you have to tip your hat to these guys. What other product has looked so good on the drawing board and resonated so intuitively with potential customers with the promise that results of a successful implementation are just around the corner? By the way, if the train track is a big circle, the corner is always just ahead of you. And to top it off, if indeed you do fail to reap the benefits, none other than Microsoft Dynamics research will inform you that it's not the system, it's your people!

Which of the following two scenarios do you think is more accurate? CRM is everything it's cracked up to be: intuitive and easy to use; completely functional as a strategic and tactical tool for advancing the sale; provides accurate analysis of the health and well being of the pipeline; provides accurate forecasting data; and has great utility to managers for assessing team and individual performance critical to their ongoing coaching efforts. Or, for the majority of sales reps and sales managers, CRM is really not much more than a burden. The state of CRM today is neither in the state of nirvana described in our first scenario, nor completely a burden. However, let's be honest. Our CRM effectiveness stinks! Isn't it time someone said it out loud?

OK, How Come it Ain't Working?

Is it the system, or is it the people? According to Microsoft Dynamics, "Sales People Fail Businesses, not CRM Systems". "It's not us, it's them!" It's understandable this kind of comment would come from a vendor isn't it? Sounds like exactly the opposite of what our friend Dr. Deming would say. The answer is: it's the system *and* the people; and one other minor detail only alluded to by Microsoft Dynamics – the process.

The research I have cited in this book, from all sources, indicates that the Pareto Principle is in full force. CSO Insights tells us that 20% of the sales team is generating 62.9% of the revenues, while 80% are generating only 37.1%. 1 in 4 (25%) sales reps use the company's formalized sales process infrequently or irregularly. Sirius Decisions says that 82% of sales reps are unprepared for meetings, indicating that less than

20% are prepared. We could go on and on. By the way, these are not new trends. So what is perpetuating these numbers? Answer: The Pareto Principle applies to any system where there is little intervention and people are essentially left to their own devices. In these systems two groups manifest themselves: the 20% who perform, and the 80% who do not. Pareto called the 20% who perform the 'Vital Few' and the other 80% the 'Trivial Many'.

Let's get back to our CRM implementation. While CRM systems have tremendous capacity and utility, they are generally non-intuitive and not very easy to use. In fact, they are designed for people who are highly organized and structured. Guess how many people fit into this category? You got it! People like me who are slightly OCD, and part of the 20% that makes up the 'Vital Few' who actually like CRM. In the meantime, for the other 80%, the 'Trivial Many' (not a pejorative but simply a term), the system is almost completely counter-intuitive, not received as beneficial, and, therefore, not adopted. Well, we'll just make them do it! Sure, that works real well. If this were the case, CRM compliance would have been 100% a long time ago. I know, let's throw some change-management methodologies at these 'Trivial Many' folks. That'll do it. Again, this has not proved to be very effective. Human nature's default is a 'left-to-their-own-devices' 80/20 Pareto System where success is dependent on the performance of a

small group of individual contributors – the 'Vital Few'.
So what's the answer?

**To Raise Performance, We Must Build a Capable System
Where The 'Trivial Many' Become The 'Capable Masses'.**

'Capable Masses' Are Built On Capable Processes.

Chapter 4

Individual Contributors vs. Capable Masses

In most sales organizations there are two groups; managers, and those who carry a bag, the 'individual contributors'. As we know from CSO Insights data, in a Pareto System there are also two groups within the individual contributors. The 20% who contribute 62.9% of sales revenues, the 'Vital Few'; and the other 80% who contribute 37.1% of sales revenues, the 'Trivial Many'. If words mean anything, we would do well to move away from the term 'individual contributor' and strive towards something like team contributor. Obviously, we need to do more than simply change our terms. What we need to do is change our culture. Let's take a quick look at the history of a company that did just that, and over the course of time changed not only their business, but the world in the process.

The Machine That Changed the World

In 1950, Toyota's manufacturing capacity was 30,000 automobiles per year. In that same year, US auto manufacturers were turning out a combined 60,000 cars per day! 57 years later in April of 2007, Toyota automobile sales surpassed that of GM. In this event, Toyota became the world's largest seller of cars. Today, Toyota produces in excess of 9.4 million vehicles per year, equivalent to one vehicle every six seconds! How did Toyota do it? More importantly; how do they continue to do it?

In 1937, Toyota Industries automobile manufacturing in Japan was founded as a spin off from the established Toyoda Spinning textile company. 52 years later, in 1989, Toyota introduced the Lexus automobile to the world. Since that time, Lexus has been known as *the* auto industry standard of quality. Additionally, the Toyota Production System, popularly know today as Lean Manufacturing, has influenced the production processes of thousands of companies around the globe. However, quality and productivity were years away from everyday practice at Toyota back in 1943 when an engineer named Taiichi Ohno joined the company.

Upon their return from a visit to Ford's River Rouge complex in 1950, Toyota executives tasked Ohno with managing a process that was very labor intensive and highly dependent on repeatability. Specifically, the assembly line process introduced by Henry Ford and  elaborated on in his book published in 1926, *Today and Tomorrow*. Despite their original intent, to learn as much as possible about process efficiency, the team actually found Ford's processes inefficient and not at all applicable to their production requirements in their plant back in Japan. It was actually on a visit to a local Piggly Wiggly where the real inspiration for TPS originated. The group noticed that when a customer purchased a product, it was almost immediately restocked with a new item. Customers were able to purchase exactly what they wanted, when they wanted it; just in time! More importantly, the store only ordered new stock, once the customer had purchased existing stock. This was in direct contrast to the massive inventory Ford was carrying to produce cars with an associated alarming amount of inefficient waste and remakes. An interesting sidebar here is that both Ford's and Ohno's inspiration originated from a common source. It was at a Chicago slaughterhouse that Ford observed the efficiencies of a continuous disassembly line that reduced a live hog to, as Philip Armour put it, *"everything but the squeal"* in less than 20 minutes. Meanwhile, there is a good chance that

Ohno walked by a display case of Armour packaged meat products during his visit to Piggly Wiggly. So you see, there is more than just a casual *link* between *sausage* and the Lexus you may be driving.

Back in Japan, Ohno architected what would become known as the Toyota Production System and quickly put his plan into practice. However, the expected results were not soon forthcoming. Apparently, Ohno's new process alone was not enough. Ohno quickly discovered that when employees did not perform to standards and expectations, the resulting variation produced poor quality resulting in expensive downtime and remakes. It was apparent to Ohno that, in order to gain control of the process, he needed trained capable workers. Moreover, Ohno realized that to meet his company's expectations he needed, not just some capable workers, but capable masses.

When Taiichi Ohno discovered the importance of capable people and capable masses, he sought a method of teaching that would support his needs. He found such a tool in the *Job Instruction (JI) Method* taught by the American Military after World War II. From this method, Ohno developed the principles of 'Standardized Work'. As the expression goes, the rest is history!

Since the 1950's, TPS, or Lean, has been the primary teaching tool for all of Toyota. Today the capabilities of Toyota employees are a hallmark of the company. And what has Toyota accomplished since 1943 with TPS and capable masses? Here are a few astounding milestones.

1950 Toyota manufactures 30,000 automobiles in a year while US auto manufacturers are producing more than 60,000 vehicles per day! Toyota implements the Toyota Production System.

1988 James Womack and his team from MIT visit Toyota facilities in Japan.

1989 Toyota introduces the Lexus ES 250.

1990 Womack publishes *"The Machine That Changed the World" The Story of Lean Manufacturing.*

2007 April 24, 2007 – Toyota surpasses GM with sales of 2.367 million automobiles!

2007 Toyota has won 103 J.D. Power Awards since 1996.

What Does Standardized Work Have to Do With the Sales Process?

Everything! Selling is fundamentally a process and therefore a perfect application for proven process improvement methodologies. In terms of process improvement, Toyota literally wrote the book! It is not surprising that the philosophy of Standardized Work (modeled after Toyota) is practiced by the largest and most successful companies around the globe. Here's what Bill Marriott, of Marriott Hotels, had to say about the relevance of Standardized Work.

"Maybe we are a little fanatical about the way things should be done. But for us, the idea of having systems and procedures for everything is natural and logical. If you want to produce a consistent result, you need to figure out how to do it, write it down, practice it, and keep improving it until there's nothing left to improve. Of course, we at Marriott believe that there's always something to improve."

One famous example of Standardized Work at Marriott is their detailed 66-step process for cleaning a room in 30 minutes or less. Can we assume that Bill Marriott would also have a rigorous set of criteria defined for such things as new hotel construction, site selection, advertising campaigns, and their corporate sales program?

According to Toyota, there are two fundamental reasons for their historical, and continual, success.

1. Relentless Reflection and Continuous Improvement.

2. People, Culture, Execution

Relentless Reflection at Toyota means that everything is measured. Not some things, not just the important things; everything! Everything is measured, and it is measured constantly. Once it is measured, it is analyzed and then improved, continually. By the way, improvement at Toyota, in most cases, does not mean dramatic improvement. In fact, in most cases, the improvements are incremental. The point is, everything is improved, diligently and continuously. Second, Relentless Reflection and Continuous Improvement is not simply a methodology or practice at Toyota; these objectives are a way of life for their people who have created a culture in which quality execution is assured. Here is a quote from a Toyota executive that best describes the point.

> *"The system requires highly capable people to maintain and continuously improve it. Merely installing the method without the appropriate development of skills and abilities will provide limited benefits, and the primary purpose of the system itself – namely increased performance through the increasing capability of people – will be lost.*
>
> *Toyota could not be successful with it's systems, TPS/ Lean. It is successful because of its people, culture and execution. Developing exceptional people is Toyota's number one priority."*

Here's a little routine you can engage in that will serve as a constant reminder of the power of learning and continual improvement. The next time you see a Lexus driving down the road, consider the Toyota Crown, the first Toyota automobile imported to the US in 1956. Then consider the introduction of the 2007 Lexus LS600h L. Finally, ask yourself, "What have I done today to improve the learning and execution of myself and my team?"

1956 Toyota Crown

**2007 Lexus LS600h L
The car that parked itself!**

Let me briefly share another well known corporate success story that was actually spawned from Toyota's early success with TPS.

It was August 1, 1989, the date of Lexus' long-awaited National Dealers Conference, the first chance for dealers to greet each other face-to-face, to meet Lexus executives from California and Japan and, at long last, to get behind the wheel of the car. As one dealer after another drove the 2.2 mile track, anxieties began evaporating as surely as the Northern California morning fog. In addition to the test drives, the weekend included rounds of golf at Pebble Beach, a lunch attended by former first lady Nancy Reagan, and presentations by confident Lexus officials.

In the most unforgettable performance, dealers were brought to an LS 400 where chief engineer Suzuki filled wine glasses stacked on the vehicle's hood with water, and then gunned the engine. The speedometer leapt from zero to 150. The water in the wine glasses remained perfectly still. "The competition has good products, but they don't have Lexus," said Bob McCurry. "You probably just made the best investment of your life." Dr. Shoichiro Toyoda, the president of Toyota Motor Corp., flew in to address the dealers. He told them, perhaps only half-jokingly, that he had decided to invest a billion dollars, and millions of hours, in a luxury car because he was tired of riding in the backs of limousines with someone else's name on them.

From the late 1970's on, Japanese quality had American manufacturers clearly back on their heels. Representative of the mounting frustration, in 1980, NBC broadcast a white paper entitled; If Japan can . . . Why can't we? Lloyd Dobyns (narrator for NBC): "We have said several times that much of what the Japanese are doing we taught them to do. And, the man who did most of the teaching is W. Edwards Deming, statistical analyst, for whom Japan's highest industrial award for quality and productivity is named. But in his own country he is not widely recognized."

The introduction of Lexus on August 1, 1989, was the culmination of almost 40 years of TPS application at Toyota. The success of Standardized Work, proven at companies such as Toyota, Marriott, Motorola, GE and scores of others is dependent on the following four executables.

1. Defining and documenting Standardized Work as Best Practices.

2. In-depth training on the established Best Practices and Standardized Work.

3. Capable execution of Critical-to-Success activities using established tools.

4. Proactive management and coaching of individuals to build capable masses that will grow and sustain sales performance.

When all four of these initiatives are brought to bear on the process, the result is the creation of capable masses and a capable organization. The following is an excerpt from the recently released book by **Jeffrey Liker** and **David Meier** *"Toyota Talent"*.

If we were to identify the single greatest difference between Toyota and other organizations (this includes service, health care, and manufacturing organizations), it would be the depth of understanding among Toyota employees regarding their work. It is our perception that most other companies detail the work process no more than 25 percent of the level achieved by Toyota. It seems to us that at most other companies there is only a superficial understanding of the work, and a great deal of uncertainty exists pertaining to the critical elements of the work. Much is left to individuals to figure out, and people make gallant efforts to produce good results. It has been our experience that in the absence of valid information, people will find some way to get the job done. Unfortunately, if everyone is figuring out something different, the resulting variation will be significant.

Let me close this section by repeating perhaps the most compelling analysis from Liker and Meier.

Toyota could not be successful with its systems only; TPS/ Lean. It is successful because of their people, culture and execution. Developing exceptional people is Toyota's number one priority."

You Cannot Hire Capable Masses

The statistics cited in the 2009 CSO report are not new. In fact, they are a chronic reality that we in sales have been dealing with for decades. However, what has changed in the past ten to fifteen years is this. In years past, product innovation, brand dominance, and market demand allowed even mediocre sales organizations to meet sales targets in spite of the 80/20 rule. Remember the expression, "You can't get fired for buying Xerox." In today's market relying on brand dominance is no longer a workable model. Parity in service and product innovation, coupled with higher market penetration by numerous capable competitive offerings, has substantially narrowed market opportunities. In the new market, the analysis shows that sales targets can not be achieved with 80/20 levels of performance. The old sales model is simply no longer viable.

Enter the life-boat drill. Last year a sales manager at a Fortune 10 company with revenues exceeding $100 billion, told me of a recently adopted performance directive. The bottom 10% of his sales force is scheduled to be terminated. Next year, again, the bottom 10% will be terminated. The Jack Welch approach has become a popular strategy for addressing low sales performance. However, what assurance does any company have that the new hires will perform any differently? The answer is very little. The 80/20 rule is ubiquitous. Therefore, it is very likely only 20% of the new 10% you are hiring will be top performers. You haven't solved the problem by simply shuffling the same old players to a different company. They're still the same people!

I learned something critical to this point through my involvement with one of the largest staffing companies in the U.S. The number one issue C-level executives face today is the hiring and retention of quality professionals. Guess why? The best people already have jobs, are doing well and aren't looking! If this is true, how many of them will be available when you decide to throw the bottom 10% of your team over the right side of the boat? In many cases you are forced to turn to the left side of the boat and pluck some other company's cast offs out of the water. Could this be one of the reasons the number of sales reps meeting or exceeding quota is only 58.8%? Hellooooo!

It's interesting that just 6 months, 1 year or 18 months prior to throwing the bottom 10% over the side we had some damn good rationale for hiring these charlatans in the first place. Oh, they were successful in their prior roles; they had experience; they fit our culture, etc., etc. At least they portrayed themselves as such. Masters of disguise was their real area of expertise. It's not us, its them…right?

Now, as I have mentioned previously, there is such a thing as a bad hire. And when you have one, those individuals need to go work somewhere else. On the other hand, is the life boat drill en mass the right strategy? While it is certainly the easy strategy, the answer is no. You cannot hire capable masses, and the lifeboat drill is not the answer to chronic under performance. The correct strategy is the creation of Capable Masses.

What About Training?
No, You Cannot Train Capable Masses

If it were possible to train Capable Masses there would have been no need to write Chapter 2 – Sales Training Doesn't Work! Next subject.

You Can Only Build Capable Masses

In my view, this is the paramount role of sales management: To build capable sales organizations by creating environments and pathways that allow the Trivial Many to be transformed into Capable Masses.

How do you build capable sales organizations and capable masses? Here's the answer in a very simple formula.

$$\boxed{C_p} + \boxed{C_m} = \boxed{C_{so}}$$

Capable Processes   *Capable Masses*   *Capable Sales Organization*

Capable Process

Build and implement best practice Capable Processes that deliver desired results when consistently executed to performance standards.

Capable Masses

Build and nurture Capable Masses in an environment where variability and inconsistency in process execution is minimized thereby empowering the majority of individuals to contribute the majority of the results vs. the 80/20 Pareto Principle.

Capable Sales Organization

Process, Capability, Learning, Execution, Accountability and Culture all combine to achieve performance expectations. In Capable Sales Organizations, training really does work!

The benefits of building a capable sales organization with Capable Processes and Capable Masses are many and profound. (By the way, building a Capable Sales Organization is the main topic in the Manager's Corner in **Series II – Shut Up & Listen... Say So What & Sell!**) In Capable Sales Organizations processes are executed with a low degree of variability. Therefore, the quality of execution is high, and defects are low. Training is leveragable and effective. Tools and principals from the training are actually utilized in the field. Best practices are leveraged across the organization. Processes are now measurable, and therefore, the root-causes of problems are more easily identified. Process improvement is more efficient. Processes with low variability are more manageable and predictable. Forecasting is therefore, highly accurate.

Conversely, in sales organizations that are not capable, processes are executed with a high degree of variability. Therefore, the quality of execution is low, and waste and defects are high. Training is not leveragable and generally ineffective. Tools and principals from the training are rarely utilized in the field. Best practices are not leveraged across the organization. Processes are not measurable, and therefore, the root-causes of problems are usually misidentified. Process improvement is highly inefficient. Processes with high variability are unmanageable and unpredictable. Forecasting is highly inaccurate. Moreover, lack of structure breeds lack of purpose and direction. Without purpose and direction, morale suffers. High turnover, voluntary and involuntary, exacts a devastating cost on sales organizations. Finally, growth tends to be sporadic and unsustainable.

Where there is structure, there is purpose and direction. The result is higher performance and higher morale as well. Organizations with Capable Masses have low turnover, higher productivity, and a lower cost of sales. Most importantly, in Capable Sales Organizations, growth is continual and sustainable over time.

OK, I'm Convinced – Let's Just Change Into A Capable Sales Organization

Not so fast my friend. There's that pesky little word 'change' you're going to have to deal with in your efforts to transform your sales organization. But this is all change for the good you say. Good or bad, changing the culture and direction of an organization can turn ugly quickly.

Why? The problem is your organization already has a culture and a direction that it is very comfortable with. But it's not working and we're not happy with it, so how could we be comfortable with it? Happy with it and comfortable with it are two different things entirely. For example, I may not be happy with the way I look, but I'm entirely comfortable with my diet which is causing me to be 20 lbs. overweight. In fact, isn't that why they call mashed potatoes and gravy comfort food? It feels good and I'm used to it. Despite the fact we may desire to lose weight, most of use are way too comfortable to change our diets, even when we know that a healthier diet would be better for us beyond just the weight loss benefits.

Our diets and the culture and direction of our sales organizations are comfortable to us even though they are detrimental to our personal and corporate wellbeing. Therefore, your organization is very likely going to want to stay in the same direction it is already headed, with the culture it already has. There's the rub! It's kind of like trying to alter the course of a large ship; extremely difficult if not impossible to do. In the next chapter I'll recall a familiar example. Remember the Titanic?

Chapter 5

Turning the Titanic: Change and the Laws of Motion

*When the harbor is calm,
all boats exhibit an equal capacity to float.*

When market conditions are favorable; when customers are in a buying mode; when credit is easy to obtain, and the harbor is calm; even loosely managed organizations, with marginally skilled sales reps, are successful. However, when market conductions are extreme, as they are currently; when customer confidence is low with an uncertain future; when credit restrictions lock out all but the most highly capitalized businesses; the harbor becomes a dangerous place where only the best managed companies with highly skilled sales reps are able to weather the storm.

We do not need to look very far for proof that in the current economic environment the harbor is anything but calm. In fact, the harbor is being battered by a surge of continuing waves that is testing all organizations' ability to float. Moreover, according to the experts, the end is not in clear sight. Most would agree that the upturn could be anywhere from 12 to 24 months away. Therefore, the critical question for management today is; how do we pilot the organization through the crisis?

In order to understand how to navigate through the storm, we must first understand the dynamics that contribute to the forward motion of an organization. Specifically, we must be aware of the forces that provide either acceleration or drag on our efforts to drive the organization to achieving sales performance objectives. In other words, to manage the process we must understand both what causes us to go faster and straighter towards our goal, as well as what causes us to go slower and further away from our goal.

Environment vs. Structure

There are two primary factors to consider. The first is the external market environment, and the second is the internal structure inherent in the organization. In our boat-in-the-harbor analogy, the external environment is the weather, and the internal structure is the boat, crew, management team and the processes in place relating to performance management. In years past, the residents of the Gulf Coast had little control over the hurricanes Mother Nature decided to hurl their way. Similarly, we too are largely unable to control the external market place and economic environment we may face at any given time. However, what is within our control is our ship, crew, management team and processes. Unfortunately, rather than proactively controlling what is within our power to control, the majority of organizations allow the environment to dictate the level of control we impose on the organization. Enter the inverse proportion rule of Environment vs. Structure illustrated in the graph below.

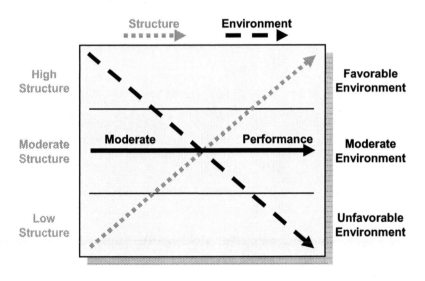

When there is a Favorable Environment and Performance expectations are being met or exceeded, the requirement for Structure tends to be Low (left side of graph above). External market conditions are good, customers are receptive, credit is easy to obtain, and even marginally skilled sales reps are selling. Management's intuitive response: "Let's not kill our momentum by imposing an inordinate amount of structure."

When there is a Moderate Environment, in order to continue to meet Performance expectations the Structure must be raised to Moderate levels (center of graph). External market conditions are fair, customers are generally receptive, credit is moderately easy to obtain, however marginally skilled sales reps are now struggling. Management's intuitive response: "Perhaps, we should impose a moderate degree of structure to apply some level of performance management to the lower performers."

When there is an Unfavorable Environment, in order to keep Performance from falling below expectations the requirements for Structure must be raised inversely to the level of the Unfavorable Environment (right side of graph). Market conditions are poor, customers are unreceptive, credit is difficult to obtain, and, even highly skilled sales reps are struggling. Management's intuitive response: "Uh oh! We need to impose a high degree of structure and apply a high level of performance management with all sales reps."

Obviously the first scenario is most desirable. The second scenario is cause for concern, and the third scenario is an all hands on deck red alert. It is in this third scenario that companies are tested in terms of their ability to mobilize their teams in the face of extreme adversity. Unfortunately, while the inverse proportion rule of Environment vs. Structure works in theory, in reality when the storm is raging applying this rule is generally not successful in achieving the desired improvements. In other words, it is extremely difficult to raise the level of structure to the required levels in times of crisis when the environment has shifted from favorable to unfavorable. Why? There is another factor to consider: cultural and structural momentum.

Newton Was a Change Management Guru

How do we explain cultural and structural momentum? Well, you'll need to stay with me and trust me for a few minutes, because we are going to introduce a concept I am sure you have never heard related to sales performance: Newton's Three Laws of Motion. "You have got to be kidding me!" No, I am not kidding you. In fact, an understanding of the physics of momentum is not simply an analogy to our current situation; it is absolutely at the core of the issue. So please, indulge me for a few more paragraphs.

Tough and unfavorable market conditions such as those we now face are, thank goodness, cyclical in nature. Therefore, the majority of time in a company's history is spent in either favorable or moderate environments. It is in these times that the cultural and structural momentum is established within an organization. I mentioned in the three scenarios above that management's response is in general intuitive. Meaning, our response to market conditions is generally reactive. Things are going well; let's not mess with it. Things are getting tougher; perhaps we should inject a bit more structure. Uh oh, things are going very badly; time to force structure into the organization. So, let's look at the graph of structure vs. environment when we take the intuitive approach in times of favorable to moderate market conditions.

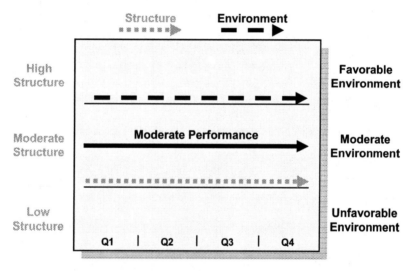

In our example the environment (black dash line) is stabilized between favorable and moderate; conditions in general are pretty good. Meaning, customers are, in most cases, receptive; credit is fairly easy to obtain; and marginally skilled sales reps are struggling just a bit. Most importantly, performance expectations are being met. Management's intuitive response: "We're doing well. The low level of structure (dotted gray line) we have is serving us well. Let's not make any dramatic changes." In these conditions, over time there may be a bad quarter here or there but there are also better than expected quarters to balance things out. The response to an anomalous bad quarter therefore is not to make dramatic changes in structure but rather to reinforce the level of structure already in place. Conversely, the response to a better than expected quarter is not to reduce the level of structure but rather maintain the current level since the overall structure is in general delivering desired performance expectations. As water seeks its own level, structure also seeks its own level requisite to the level of prosperity.

Over the course of time, in this case four quarters, the level of structure in the organization is fairly stable. Add a few previous years of similar results, and we could say the level of structure is very stable. In fact, by this time the level of structure is now established as a culture within the organization. This is where we begin to apply the laws of motion.

Newton's First Law of Motion states the following:

An object at rest tends to stay at rest, and an object in motion tends to stay in motion with the same speed, and in the same direction, unless acted upon by an unbalanced force.

In other words, once a culture of structure has been established over time, it takes on the properties of an object in motion. Meaning, whatever the level of structure that has been established, the culture and momentum of that structure will tend to maintain its level, and motion, in a straight line, unless some unbalancing force changes the direction. Want some proof? Every organization that has been in existence for an extended period of time has a culture associated with it. We have all experienced this first hand in our professional lives. How difficult is it to change the culture in an established organization? Without dramatic and disruptive change, it is almost impossible. It's the old expression used to describe how hard it is to execute change: "It's like trying to turn a battleship." Why? Because the battleship has tremendous momentum, and Newton's law states that the battleship will therefore tend to resist change and stay in motion at the same speed and direction it is headed. This, by the way, is a core principle in the discipline of Change Management; change is not easy because the status quo has momentum.

How much momentum does the cultural structure in an organization have? Newton's Second Law of Motion talks about force (cause) acceleration (effect), and mass (size).

Force = Mass X Acceleration

When the level of structure becomes a culture, it has the Force of the entire organization behind it. The larger the size of the organization, the larger the Mass.

The stronger the Force, and the larger the Mass, the greater the Acceleration. Most organizations cannot be accused of moving too quickly in anything, so acceleration, or speed, is not really a consideration. What is a consideration is the force of the culture, and the mass, or size, of the organization. Back to our battleship analogy. It would be fairly easy to turn a 10' metal row boat weighing 80 lbs traveling at 10 knots. Dip and hold one oar in the water and the boat turns! By the way, 1 knot is 1.15077945 miles per hour. However, an 874' long battleship weighing 44,638 tons, or 89,276,000 lbs, traveling at the same 10 knots, would be exponentially more difficult to turn. Try hanging off the side, dip an oar in the water, and see what happens: nothing!

Let's get back to our Structure vs. Environment chart, and see what happens when things change, and how the momentum of culture and structure affects the organization. Here's the scenario. The environment has turned unfavorable. Market conditions are poor, customers are unreceptive, credit is difficult to obtain, and, even highly skilled sales reps are struggling. Management's intuitive response: "Uh oh! We need impose a high degree of structure and apply a high level of performance management with all sales reps." The previous market conditions of moderate to favorable environments have long since established a culture of structure within the organization relating to performance management. This culture has a definite momentum in terms of force and mass; the whole organization has done it this way for a long time. With sales performance in steady decline, management intuitively attempts to change things by imposing more structure relating to sales activities in a number of areas.

- Business Development
- Qualifying
- Call Activity
- Needs Analysis
- Reporting and Compliance in CRM
- Justification
- Accuracy of Data in CRM
- Time Management
- Pipeline Management
- Forecasting

While well intended, management is also part of, and subject to, the culture that has been established in the organization. Meaning, despite the urgency of the situation, the objectives above are delivered in much the same spirit as before. "Hey people, these are the things we need to do to turn things around. Let's grab hold of these and do our best with them. Go team!"

What should be presented as all-hands-on-deck-must-do directives are instead presented as strongly worded suggestions. "It's not our culture to be too heavy handed about these things. Our folks are professionals, and they will do the right thing." I think you can guess what happens, as illustrated by the following graph.

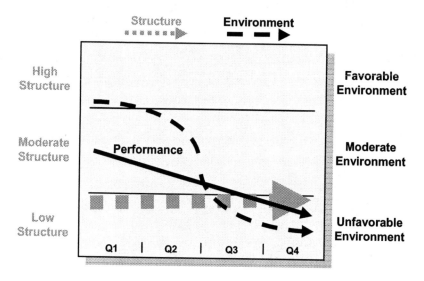

The unfavorable environment, dash black line, has reduced performance, solid black line, well below expectations. Despite all efforts to raise the level of structure, the cultural momentum (heavy gray dash line) resists changing its level and direction. If there is any change, it is incremental. The result is without increased structure relating to more consistent business development, more accurate qualifying, increased call activity, more effective needs analysis, higher compliance in regard to CRM reporting and accuracy of data, better justification of the solution, increased levels of time management, more comprehensive pipeline management, and, the big daddy of them all, more accuracy in forecasting, not much changes. As a result performance continues to go down, or stagnates, at an unacceptable level. With no appreciable improvement both management and staff become beleaguered and frustrated. Alternative measures to boost profitability include dramatic cost cutting along with a loss of jobs from the front line reps all the way to the executive level. The inability to control the internal structure leaves the company completely at the mercy of the external environment. If market conditions do not improve, the consequences will be dire.

Following are some alarming statistics compiled from subject matter experts (ranging from the *Harvard Business Review* to the *Journal of Change Management*) that illustrate the inability to control the cultural and structural momentum in organizations.

- Two-thirds of Total Quality Management (TQM) programs fail, and reengineering initiatives fail 70% of the time (Senge, 1999, pp. 5-6).

- Top-down organizational change programs have a poor record of success (Beer, 2003, p. 626).

- A seminal study found a 64% failure rate among new technological innovations introduced into municipal public service programs (Yin, 1978, p. vi).

- A decision to adopt an innovation does not automatically lead to implementation (Rogers, 1995, p. 371).

- Change initiatives crucial to organizational success fail 70% of the time (Miller, 2002, p. 360).

- Major corporate investments in technology are not used as intended or abandoned within six months 80% of the time (Gartner Group in Miller, 2002, p. 360).

- Of 100 companies that attempted to make fundamental changes in the way they did business, only a few were very successful (Kotter, 1995, p. 59).

- Leaders of the corporate reengineering movement report that the success rate for Fortune 1000 companies is below 50%, possibly only 20% (Strebel, 2000, p. 86).

- Companies that successfully implement a strategic plan are a minority, with estimates ranging from 10% to 30% (Raps, 2004, p. 49).

- Implementation of innovations has historically had a high failure rate (Majchrzak in Linton, 2001, p. 65).

- Management history is littered with failed innovation programs (e.g., TQM, quality circles, Reengineering, and job enrichment) that started with a bang but fizzled out. (Repenning, 2002, p. 109).

- Most organizational change programs fail or have limited success because they are guided by an erroneous theory about how to bring about change. Most begin with a bang, but go out with a whimper (Argyris, 1990, p. 4; Beer, Eisenstat, & Spector, 1990a, 1990b).

Not encouraging at all! So, how do we counter and effectively change the direction of the cultural and structural momentum within our organizations? Enter Newton's Third Law of Motion.

For every action, there is an equal, and opposite, reaction.

Let's apply this to our battleship scenario. In order to change the cultural and structural momentum within our organization, we must apply an equal force of change in an opposite or tangent direction. For example, if our 80 lb, 10' long row boat ran head long into our 44,638 ton battleship, how much would the battleship slow down? There would be no noticeable change in speed or direction. However, if our 44,638 ton battleship ran head long into another 44,638 ton battleship, each traveling at 10 knots, both ships would stop immediately and of course in the process destroy each other from the tremendous force of the impact. Destruction is obviously not our objective. However, we are looking to dramatically change the direction of the ship. Enter the diminutive by comparison tug boat, designed with an incredible amount of power for its size so it can do one thing; turn battleships and cruisers in a short amount of time and distance. The bigger and more powerful the tug, the more quickly the turn can be executed. A 44,638 ton tug could turn our battleship virtually on a dime.

There are two approaches to changing momentum: Apply a smaller force, which requires a greater amount of time and distance, or, apply a greater force which requires less time and distance to change direction. Clearly there are volumes written on the subject of change management. Which then is the proper approach to use? Obviously, it is a question of the time and distance available. In times of prosperity, the approach of less force, the kinder and gentler approach let's call it, is appropriate. After all things are going well, and we have time and distance to change the cultural and structural momentum. However, in times of crisis, when there is clear and present danger, the approach of less force is completely ineffective.

A Titanic Lesson – Change Direction Now!

It was April 14, 1912. The Titanic was on her maiden voyage from Southampton, England to New York. "At 11:35 p.m., the lookouts spotted a massive iceberg less than a quarter of a mile off the bow of the ship. Immediately, the engines were thrown into reverse and the rudder turned hard left. Because of the tremendous *mass* (Newton's momentum) of the ship, slowing and turning took an incredible distance, more than that available. Five minutes later, at 11:40 p.m., without enough distance to alter her course, the Titanic sideswiped the iceberg, damaging nearly 300 feet of the right side of the hull above and below the waterline. In less than 3 hours, at 2:29 a.m., the bow of the Titanic struck the bottom of the ocean." [Gannon, 1995]. Newton's three laws of motion explain the physics behind the sinking of the Titanic.

Applying the Formula

How then should sales organizations apply the laws of motion to their current situation? Quite simply, the force of change in an organization must be requisite to alter the existing cultural and structural momentum of the organization within the time and distance available to avoid the disaster of crashing into the iceberg. In my estimation, given the current unfavorable environment and expectations from shareholders, that equates to 90 days or one operating quarter. That does not mean that in 90 days we will have solved the problem and performance will leap up to expectations. What it does mean is that in 90 days we will be applying the requisite force to counter the current cultural and structural momentum and begin to turn the ship in the direction of improved levels of structure and performance.

Where do we begin? We must first understand, and expect, resistance to our change initiatives. Resistance to change is equivalent to the Force component in our equation. The number of employees exerting this Force, or resistance, is equivalent to the Mass. Obviously, it is easier to counter the resistance of one individual than that of the entire organization; in change management there truly is strength in numbers.

Why do employees resist change? Here are 10 reasons from A. J. Schuler, Psy. D.

Top Ten Reasons People Resist Change:

1. The risk of change is seen as greater than the risk of standing still. *Fear of the unknown.*

2. People feel connected to other people who are identified with the old ways. *We are creatures of habit, and birds of a feather stick together.*

3. People have no role models for the new activity. *Fear there will be no support system.*

4. People fear they lack the competence to change. *Fear of failure.*

5. People feel overloaded and overwhelmed. *Fear of losing control.*

6. People have a healthy skepticism and want to be sure new ideas are sound. *Unwillingness to learn because they see no obvious need.*

7. People fear hidden agendas among would-be reformers. *Lack of trust.*

8. People feel the proposed change threatens their notion of themselves. *Fear of personal impact.*

9. People anticipate a loss of status or quality of life. *Protection of one's territory.*

10. People genuinely believe that the proposed change is a bad idea. *Closed minded; the new way may not be better.*

The greater the resistance to change the greater the Force component of the cultural and structural momentum. John P. Kotter, with the *Harvard Business Review*, says: "Dealing with resistance is crucial to successful change management…" Robert Kegan and Lisa Laskow Lahey, also with the *Harvard Business Review*, wrote the following: "So what is the real reason people won't change? To bottom line it, it's a psychological dynamic called a 'competing commitment,' and until managers understand how it works and the ways to overcome it, they can't do a thing about change-resistant employees. When people resist change, it's not necessarily because they're opposed to it. It's not even necessarily because they're lazy or inattentive to it, either. Rather, it's because they have one or more hidden beliefs that directly conflict with them working toward meaningful change."

Hidden beliefs, hidden agendas, not so hidden beliefs and agenda; resistance to change is real. The inability to control this dynamic, in terms of managing change as shown by the failure rate of change initiatives mentioned previously, is even more real.

Ironically, dealing with change during a time of crisis, the storm in the harbor, actually presents us with a unique opportunity not available to us in times of more favorable environments. When times are good, people feel that change is unnecessary: "If it ain't broke don't fix it." What is lacking in times of prosperity is a sense of urgency for change. Therefore, people have the luxury of time to mull over how they will either accept or resist change. In times when people perceive that 'it ain't broke', Robert J. Kriegel's offers sound advice in his book *"If It Ain't Broke, Break It!"*

Urgency is a tremendous motivator. When John P. Kotter, with the *Harvard Business Review*, outlined 8 critical stages leaders must manage to give change transformation the best chance of succeeding, at the top of the list was "Establish a sense of urgency". Again, in times of prosperity, without a sense of urgency people have the luxury of indulging in a deep dive into the 10 reasons why they should not change. On the other hand, in times of crisis there is inherent urgency. It is in these times that people look for a leader to rise above the chaos and take control. It's called the herding instinct. Sometimes you hear the expression circling the wagons. It is true that times of crisis actually provide us with unique opportunities to leverage the inherent urgency by exhibiting strong leadership to mobilize the team in one direction with a common cause to accomplish the change goals.

With strong leaders and leadership, another behavioral response to crisis can work in our favor to accomplish change. It is called 'emulation'. In times of crisis, some members of the group will mimic the behavior of other members with higher status. "Ain't that the truth!" Obviously this can work against us as well. For example, there is a time of crisis. People are looking to a leader for leadership. The leader offers a lot of talk and motivation about how we are all going to run through the fire. Finally, the leader says, "OK team. Go for it and I'll you see when you get back." All of a sudden there are not too many people enthused about running through the fire when the leader is sitting back at the camp sipping a latte. The emulated behavior becomes, "I'll sit down as well and do nothing." Leaders who are prepared to actually lead are able to leverage the dynamics of human behavior during a crisis and accomplish great things. For those willing to lead, Kotter's eight stages provide a sound roadmap for execution.

1. Establish a sense of urgency.

2. Form a powerful guiding coalition to lead the effort.

3. Create a vision to direct the change initiative.

4. Communicate the vision using every vehicle possible.

5. Empower others to act on the vision; for example, by encouraging risk taking.

6. Create short-term wins (visible performance improvements) to whip up enthusiasm.

7. Consolidate performance improvements and produce more change.

8. Institutionalize new approaches developed during the initiative.

Following is a 90 day strategic plan for getting your change initiative started.

90-Day Strategic Plan

1. Establish a sense of urgency. Sound the alarm and mobilize the troops.

- Articulate the current situation, challenges, and problems as well as the impact on the business both short and long term.

- Schedule a launch initiative conference call to the organization from each executive; CEO, CFO, President, CMO, HR and Operations. 5 to 10 minutes from each executive will require a 1 hour call.

- Sales managers should then schedule a 30 minute call with their teams, to further articulate the urgency of the current situation.

2. Form a powerful guiding coalition to lead the effort. Identify who will lead the charge.

- The executive team provides the vision, guidance, and the plan.

- The sales managers will lead and be responsible for execution.

- Sales managers will be empowered to enlist the assistance from the executive team as needed.

3. Create a vision to direct the change initiative. Define where we are headed, how we will get there and what will be the benefit of success.

- The executive and management teams should craft a strategic and tactical plan detailing timelines, benchmarks, expectations, and resource allocation.

- The vision and guidance should reiterate the cost of failure and the benefit of success.

4. Communicate the vision using every vehicle possible. "It's everywhere I look."

- The vision and guidance should be published in hard copy and mailed to every A/E.

- Schedule a monthly conference call from an executive to update progress.

- Send out a weekly e-mail message from the President and the CEO to reinforce vision and guidance.

- Conduct weekly forecast calls with sales managers to qualify and quantify team and individual progress.

- Weekly reporting from CRM should also support the initiative.

5. **Empower others to act on the vision. Follow the directive to meet objectives, take calculated risks to exceed them.**

   - The company's expectation is that everyone will execute the directives.

   - The company's hope is that everyone will exceed expectations by taking calculated risks.

   - Therefore, failure to act is unacceptable. However, failure after thoughtful and diligent execution creates an opportunity for encouragement and coaching for better future results.

6. **Create short-term wins to whip up enthusiasm. Set the bar progressively higher.**

   - Management should set short-term weekly achievable goals to create the short-term wins necessary to build enthusiasm and motivate the team.

   - The bar for these goals should get progressively higher with each week in order to achieve final 90 day objectives.

   - Share the wins with the entire organization. Recognition promotes individual and team motivation.

7. Consolidate performance improvements and produce more change. Build on success.

- First comes vision and guidance, then motivation, then execution, then success. What follows, is an opportunity for greater vision, greater motivation, greater execution and greater success.

- Leverage success to create greater success.

8. Institutionalize new approaches developed during the initiative. Be fluid and adaptable to plan accelerators.

- Vision and guidance establish the goal and the road map. Along the way creative ideas for accelerating the process will emerge from the team. These accelerators should be embraced and institutionalized into the operating plan.

- If the new approach is not an accelerator, or it is outside the scope of the vision and guidance, it should be dismissed.

Critical Success Factor for Kotter's Eight Stages:

Change Starts At The Top!

Chapter 6

Solutions

If I were to talk about solutions at this point without first presenting a compelling business case, every one of the participants in my past training sessions would call me out on the 'context' carpet. "Presenting your business case is like telling a story..." I tell to them. "Don't tell your solution story out of the context of the business need. And, the customer's story, their business needs, is Chapter 1." So before we talk about solutions, let's review the business case from your perspective. We're close to the end of the book so we'll keep it short and to the point. By the way, the numbers in the business case are courtesy of our friends at CSO Insights.

The Business Case From Your Perspective

Current State:

The experts, CSO Insights and others, say our sales productivity stinks. And, the trend over the past few years has been flat with 2009 performance being slightly down. In other words, it ain't getting any better. So, as we have shown by comparison to the level of performance achieved in other areas of the business, the experts are right.

At this point I'm going to throw in a little something called **So What!** from the upcoming Series II. In fact, let's just do this as a little role play. I'll ask the questions, and of course, I'll answer for you too, if you don't mind.

The numbers clearly show that our sales productivity stinks. **So What!** *So what problems is this situation creating for you?*

Problems:

That's an easy one to answer. There's just one problem. We're not hitting our sales targets! By the way, in my job, nothing else matters.

I understand. But **So What!** *What does it matter if you don't hit your numbers? Hey, it's tough out there and everyone is struggling to hit their numbers. How is this problem impacting the business, your team, and you?*

Impact:

Well, I've had to fire 13.1% of my sales force. Another 15.3% left voluntarily. Last week I had to fire a rep who had been with the company for 26 years. He not only worked for me, he was a friend. That was not a pleasant situation for anyone. As a company we missed our numbers last quarter. As a result our CEO and VP of Sales were just fired. Oh, and they decided to reduce the number of sales territories…again. So, I just inherited another region and a good friend of mine, and fellow manager, is now unemployed. The new management is putting more pressure than ever on me and my team. Since only 58.8% of my reps are at or exceeding quota, almost half of my team is not making any money right now. They are just ecstatic about that…not! Yes, along with the economy and the tough market, morale is at an all time low. I'm working harder than ever to meet my personal and team quota. Last Thursday I missed my daughter's birthday and Friday night I missed my son's homecoming football game. One last thing, with the current state of my marriage my wife and I are good candidates for the Dr. Phil show.

*Sounds tough! But again…***So What!*** At least you still have a job. So you had to fire someone. You know some people really shouldn't be on the bus in the first place, right? Get rid of the dead weight, lean up, and move on. There is one question however. What's going to happen if nothing changes in the next 3 to 6 to 12 months? What will be the consequences if you fail to change the current situation?*

The Consequences of Inactivity:

Boy, you really have a knack for asking the obvious questions. If nothing changes, I'll probably be the next one to get fired! It's that simple.

OK, let me ask you this. On a scale of 1 to 10, how would you gauge your level of urgency for a solution to your problem of poor sales productivity?

Level of Urgency for a Solution:

Another easy one. That would be a 10.

I understand. So what would be the benefit to the company, your team and you if you actually did improve sales performance? What would be the specific benefits of a solution?

The Benefit of a Solution:

Well, first of all, I wouldn't get fired. Second, I wouldn't have to fire any more of my team and hope that I hired productive sales reps in their place. Third, the company would meet their revenue projections and therefore we wouldn't miss our forecast to Wall Street. Meaning, our new VP of Sales won't get fired. More sales would benefit the entire organization supporting our selling efforts. Our executives would be happy, our shareholders would be happy, our customers would be happy, my family and I would be happy, etc, etc. Obviously, more sales would cure a multitude of problems.

Now that sounds like a much more desirable picture then the one where everyone is getting fired. So what and where are the gaps you need to bridge in order to achieve the far more desirable state of success?

The Gaps:

Now that question is not an easy one is it. We've got marketing campaigns but 52.3% of the leads my team generates are through their own efforts. We've got a CRM application but my team doesn't use it like they should because they don't see it as a helpful tool. In fact, only 20.2% of them say CRM helps them improve their win rates. Only 16.1% say CRM shortens the sales cycle. Of course they are not the only ones to blame for the failure of CRM. Most of my peers, 72% of the sales managers, and I tolerate insufficient use and application of the CRM tool in our selling efforts.

We have a sales process but like most companies, 62.8% of them, our adherence to the process is random and informal. In fact, when I asked them, my reps told me that execution of our sales process is only a 22.2% factor in winning deals. Now, that is not to say that we don't have a few sales stars working here who are doing all the right things. Lord knows I wish we had more than just 20% of our top reps generating 61.5% of our total revenues. The problem is like a lot of companies, 46.7%, we don't seem to be very good at sharing the best practices of these top reps across the organization. Of course we have sales training. We invest on average $1,500 per rep per year in training. The problem is that like most companies, a full 70%, we do not consistently apply the sales methodology taught in class when we get back in the field. Probably something to do with that applying best practices thing again. Like a lot of companies, 50%, I would say that the training is not meeting our expectations.

I suppose if we look at it from our customer's perspective, like 40.6% of other companies, we probably need to do a better job at understanding our customer's buying process. I suppose that's why our customers say that 3 out of 4 sales calls are a waste of time and 82% of our sales reps are unprepared for meetings.

Wow! Quite a list of gaps you've got there. But I still have to say **So What!** *So what if your reps and your processes and your systems and your training and your managing are...well... incapable?*

Well, the so what to your question is only 48% of the deals we forecast actually close. And therefore only 58.8% of our reps are meeting or exceeding quota.

Given the level 10 urgency you said you have for a solution, how would you describe the solution that you need to have in place to achieve your objectives? What are the Critical Success Factors?

Critical Success Factors:

I need to close every one of the gaps I just outlined. In order to do that I need three things. First, I need to identify the most effective selling methodologies; the best practices. Second, I need all of my team, not just 20%, executing these best practices consistently and to performance standards. Third, I absolutely must have a framework to ensure sustainable and consistent results over time. That's it! Simple solution, right?

Simple to say; yes. Simple to do? Now that's the toughest question in this whole dialogue.

Solutions:

If you are sufficiently charred from the burning platform we have created in our Manager's Corner, let me offer some relief by sharing some of the solutions we will be detailing in Series II. We mentioned back in Chapter 1 that the first step in any 12-step recovery program is admitting there is a problem. I hope you are at this point up to your eyeballs in step 1 and now at a point of readiness to move on.

Seizing control of your sales leadership destiny is not a 12-step program. It is instead an elegant 3-Step plan. The context is the three Critical Success Factors we have just outlined; best practices, execution to performance standards, and sustainable results over time. Our objective is to rise above the current state.

- The majority of sales organizations view Best Practices as Best Suggestions...*at Best!*

- In the absence of Best Practice standards and largely left to their own devices, sales managers and their teams have resorted to the best of intentions approach.

- Despite everyone "doing their best", the result is a lack of discipline and consistency in sales process execution and performance.

- Without a structured approach to selling it is difficult to identify success facilitators or inhibitors. As a result, best practices remain unleveraged while ineffective practices are perpetuated.

- As best intention strategies continue to fail to produce results, the sales strategy soon deteriorates into one of *"Everyone Needs to Just Pedal Faster!"*

- Rather than producing greater results, pressurizing the system instead causes the weak links in the system to fail and break. Ultimately the organization finds itself chronically bound and constrained by Pareto's 80/20 rule: A small group of vital individuals produce the majority of sales results while the trivial many struggle to contribute.

Our objective is to achieve the desired state shown below in our success formula outlined in Chapter 4 of the Manager's Corner.

$$\boxed{C_p} + \boxed{C_m} = \boxed{C_{so}}$$

Capable Processes *Capable Masses* *Capable Sales Organization*

How do we get there? That's our 3-step solution.

▶ Intelligent ▶ Directive ▶ Control®

<h2>

$\boxed{C_p}$ How Do We Implement Capable Processes?
</h2>

Hope and *'Pedaling Faster'* is not a strategy. An ▶ **Intelligent** system identifies successful activities and practices, and then leverages those practices into learning that benefits the entire organization. This is the framework required to establish Best Practice processes and standards.

<h2>

$\boxed{C_m}$ How Do We Build Capable Masses?
</h2>

As we said in Chapter 4, by first understanding you cannot hire capable masses. If this were possible you would have already done so. Second, you cannot create capable masses with training 'events'. As we know, the expert's analysis reveals that despite significant investments in sales training we continue to experience poor sales performance quarter to quarter, year to year.

Capable masses are built and nurtured in ▶ **Directive** environments where variability and inconsistency in process execution is minimized. To ensure performance standards are achieved, Critical-to-Success activities are managed as Performance Directives, not suggestions or electives. Best Practices are exploited ensuring continual and sustained improved team performance.

C_{SO} How Do We Become A Capable Sales Organization?

By employing an effective ▶ **Control** system that focuses on managing process activities versus process outcome. When process activities are consistently managed over time, the probability of success across the organization is maximized. The result is a capable sales organization. Capable Sales Organizations are built and sustained on:

- ▶ **Intelligent** Processes
- ▶ **Directive** Management Approaches
- ▶ **Controlled** Performance Environments

Manager's Corner

Chapter 7

Wrap Up

In this first series we have taken a hard and honest look at the current state of sales management in a number of critical areas. Despite the sobering statistics, I am convinced there is cause for great hope. Why? The solution to our problems is directly ahead of us and certainly within our grasp. We have at our disposal a proven methodology that has the power to transform our sales organizations into capable masses. Toyota, Motorola, GE and scores of other successful organizations have provided us with a practical blueprint:

Reduce variability and improve quality through standardized work. Implement effective controls to ensure sustained performance and continual improvement over time.

There is absolutely no reason or excuse to perpetuate the status quo. Only three obstacles stand in the way of our success; old thinking, entrenched cultures that resist change, and…you. Yes my friends, we managers are a huge part of the problem. Unfortunately, too many of us think it's everything and everyone else. Perhaps we can all learn a lesson from one manager who had the courage and insight to accept responsibility for his team's success *and* failures.

In early 2007, I led a training session for sales managers in San Diego. The content of the session focused on how to better manage your team's opportunity generation efforts. All of the manager's teams had previously been through the basic opportunity generation course and were subsequently executing live opportunity generation campaigns in the field. Unfortunately, execution in practice was not as successful as expected. Hence, the follow up session for the managers on how to improve results.

To kick-off the class, I stood at the flip chart in front of the room and asked the following 'burning platform' question: "Why are your teams' opportunity generation efforts falling short of expectations?" Here are some of the answers I recorded.

- They start a campaign and don't finish it.

- There's no follow through.

- Some people are just too unorganized to successfully execute the entire plan.

- In many cases they try once and fail. Once they have failed they give up and don't try again.

- Messaging: The wrong message to the wrong audience.

- Too narrow a focus in terms of product and target audience.

- Too broad a focus in terms of product and target audience.

There were a few more bullet points, but you get the idea. I paused for a moment to review the list and then turned to the room and said the following. "Wow! That's quite a list of reasons why your teams are unsuccessful in their efforts. However, let me ask you a pointed question. Is it even remotely possible that the reason your teams are failing in their efforts…is because you allow them to fail?" There was a tangible silence in the room as they stared at the list and processed my question. Finally, one brave manager in the back of the room began shaking his head in agreement and said, "You know what Dave, you're right. We certainly own our share of the blame." That same manager wrote the following comment on his course evaluation: "I came here thinking this class was about my team. It was about me!"

Let me share one last story to wrap up the Manger's Corner. Remember my CEO friend who was fired? Well, the incoming CEO asked me to deliver a session on forecasting at the upcoming kick-off meeting that January. The sessions went very well and that evening they had scheduled the awards dinner honoring those who had performed above and beyond in the previous year. Just after dinner and prior to the awards, the CEO and I were engaged in conversation in the back of the ballroom. By the way, as is usual, a number of sales reps had been terminated, life-boated, just prior to the meeting (No sense paying travel and expenses for individuals who were soon to be ushered off the bus). The CEO asked me a question as he motioned to the tables of sales reps finishing their meals. "Dave, so what do you think of this team? Can they get us there?" Meaning, can this team of sales reps get us to our sales targets. Without hesitation I answered. "This team can definitely get you there. However, the sales team is not your problem. It's your management team that has the potential to kill you." His response was a nod of tacit approval; the point is understood or implied without being stated openly. As expected, the following year's programs were entirely focused on the sales reps with literally no emphasis on improving management effectiveness.

My question is, as managers, why aren't we stating the problem more openly? Art Sundry had the guts to say it out in the open; "Our Quality Stinks!" The expert's analysis is telling us our sales productivity stinks and if we're honest, we have to agree with them. But what about how *we* are *managing?* Are we exempt? How long are we going to continue to deflect the responsibility for the failure of our sales teams? Again, is it even remotely possible that the reason our teams fail in their efforts…is because we allow them to fail?

When do we allow our people to fail? When we fail to direct them to win! How? By accepting rampant variability and poor quality. By failing to leverage proven best practices. By promoting individual approaches over standardized work. By abandoning effective controls to ensure sustained performance and continual improvement over time. By leaving our teams to their own devices and then expecting them to meet performance standards. "Hey if they don't sell, we've still got that fire hire and train program. It's not us, it's them…right?" Is it?

But Dave, we're all doing our best. There's no question we're all well intentioned. However, we now know that doing our best is not good enough. We need to know what to do, and then do our best. In the Series II Manager's Corner, we'll take a deep dive into the ▶ **Intelligent** ▶ **Directive** ▶ **Control** methodology. In the meantime, we find ourselves back at step 1 of the 12 steps; acknowledging that we have a chronic and persistent problem that we are incapable of fixing on our own. Are you there yet? If so, you're ready for the Series II Manager's Corner.

Quest *for* Success Directives

Quest *for* Success Directive #1:
The road to sales success is about you and nothing else
because nothing else is truly in your control!

Stop Trying to Change Things
That Are Not In Your Control!

Quest *for* Success Directive #2:
Waiting is not a strategy!

Stop Waiting for Change!

Quest *for* Success Directive #3:
Playing the blame game is just an excuse for failure.

Stop Blaming Everything & Everyone Else!

Quest *for* Success Directive #4:
Are you in control of your sales destiny?

Start Taking Control of Your Sales Destiny
By Changing What You Can - Yourself!

Quest *for* Success Directive #5:
Put away your crying towel,

Stop Whining & Sell!

Quest *for* **Success Directive #6:**
Making sales calls is your #1 objective. All other activities are subordinate to this categorical imperative.
Make More Sales Calls!

Quest *for* **Success Directive #7:**
Stop waiting in line for the elevator to success.
Be Willing to Take the Stairs!

Quest *for* **Success Directive #8:**
If it's not in your schedule, it's not real. Plan to win!
Schedule Everything!

Quest *for* **Success Directive #9:**
Stop engaging in activities that are clearly not your job or your responsibility. Just say NO! Be professional.
Be a Facilitator, Not a Fixer!

Quest *for* **Success Directive #10:**
Make a list, just say no.
Pay Yourself First!

Quest *for* **Success Directive #11:**
"Your family, your religion, and the Green Bay Packers."
Prioritize! Delegate! Make Time!

Quest *for* **Success Directive #12:**
The road to hell is paved with good intentions.
Get an Accountability Partner!

Quest *for* **Success Directive #13:**
Activity for activity's sake is a waste of valuable time.
Engage in Qualified Activity!

Quest *for* **Success Directive #14:**
Selling outside of your space diminishes sales success.
Sell In Your Sweet Spot!

Quest *for* **Success Directive #15:**
Everyone is *not* a prospect.
Real Prospects Meet
Your Customer Qualifying Criteria!

Quest *for* **Success Directive #16:**
Develop You 'Sixth Sense'.
Stop Hanging Out With Dead People!

About the Author

Dave has 30 years of sales, marketing, and management experience having worked for several industry leading global companies in various capacities as Senior Sales Executive, Regional Director of Sales, National Sales Manager, National Account Manager, National Marketing Manager, Global Sales Channel Manager and Vice President of Creative Services.

Dave has received numerous awards for outstanding sales performance including Blue Chip Club membership at 173% of quota in his first year of selling, followed by multiple Presidents' Club honors as a sales executive and sales manager.

In 1982, Dave founded and served as President of Atlanta Graphic Services, a full service marketing and communications production company. Employing 36 people and in operation for 8 years, the AGS account list included the likes of Delta Air Lines, Georgia Pacific, Bell South, Atlanta Magazine, The International Association of Financial Planners along with a host of Atlanta's largest advertising agencies.

Dave's sales facilitating career began in 1995 as a SPIN® Selling certified instructor. Since that time he has trained thousands of sales professionals and managers in training sessions in the United States, Canada, Europe, India, China, Southeast Asia and Australia. Areas of expertise and training certification include sales process, sales skills development, business development, collaborative selling, account management excellence, effective coaching, change management, sales negotiating and effective sales management.

Dave is also an experienced practitioner of Lean Six-Sigma process improvement methodologies. In 2006, Dave completed his Six Sigma® Green Belt training at Motorola University in Schaumburg, IL. In 2009, he completed his Six Sigma Black Belt training at the Georgia Institute of Technology in Atlanta, GA. Dave attended Rutgers University in Newark, NJ.

Dave currently resides in Kennesaw, GA with his wife and 5 children.

Testimonials & Letters

David Danielson is one of the most creative and inventive sales professionals I have had the privilege of working with. His ability to make the complex simple, the theoretical practical, and what is at times incomprehensible understandable is exemplary.

David and I have worked together helping some of the world's most successful sales professionals and account managers achieve even greater levels of success.

If you are in sales or sales leadership, David's insight and ability to enlighten makes this book a must read.

DC – Global Sector Leader & Partner, West Midlands, UK

I feel with Dave's many years of hardcore selling experience, and equal time spent teaching, this book will help sales professionals focus on what is most important to the customer. It will be a boon for anyone who is looking to increase their productivity in these difficult times.

Bhartesh Jamdade – Sales Manager, Mumbai, India

When I was a new sales rep I never had the benefit of a tool like *The Seven Steps for Taking Control of Your Sales Destiny*. However after attending Dave's training sessions, I immediately took a quantum leap in sales comprehension. In fact, working with Dave's methodologies helped me become last year's #1 sales consultant in North America in every product category and despite the terrible economic crisis we are now experiencing.

If you truly want to make *real money* and *quota*, Dave's method *REALLY WORKS!*

I heartily endorse this superb selling series as it will keep me consistently rich, on top, and happy, over and over again.

Many thanks to Dave Danielson for creating such a wonderful sales tool.

Langford Meredith – President, Top Salesmen Club of America

After 27 years as a senior sales executive with the same company, in essentially the same territory, I thought I knew everything! That was before I begin participating in Dave's classes. Dave's sessions have definitely helped me in the areas of gaining a difficult appointment, advancing the sale, and most importantly, closing the sale. Now, I carry a 'Needs Discovery Survey Sheet' and 'Engage & Advance Worksheet' into every new account I call on.

JH – Atlanta, GA

One thing I can say about Dave's book is it really gives you that 'Ah-ha' experience. The struggle with sales, trying different things, getting tired of the uphill struggle to make targets, wishing you can just understand a small part of what is really going on and get some traction. This is where Dave's 'Ah ha' moment comes in; placing things in prospective focusing on the things that are really important and producing results with an easy action plan.

This is by no means a quick fix but it is extremely liberating when one negotiates the struggle for growth in sales on a strong foundation. I'm sure this book will get you to say "Ah ha…Now it's all a lot clearer."

Cornell Swart – CEO and Entrepreneur, Sandton, South Africa

Dave,

I could not be any more proud of what we are accomplishing after having read some of the success stories from the sales organization. I truly believe we can get all of our people to understand and use this process. Let's keep providing the tools and educating the team and I am confident the victories will drive even greater usage.

Thanks again Dave for the energy you put into this program.

Mark – President, Americas Region

Dave,

The sales training is helping our team become highly focused. When they see that these tools are resulting in real sales, it makes everyone strive for excellence. At the end of the day, you are making my job easier as it helps my region achieve personal and team targets.

Thanks again for your training program. I can see a noticeable difference in the professionalism, performance and level of desire across the board.

Todd – Sales Director, Canada

Dave,

No matter where I work, no matter what industry, no matter what era, this is how I will think, sell, and ultimately succeed as I go forward from now on! Do you think I'm just a bit excited to get up in the morning and go to work now? You bet your life!! I get chills just thinking about it! No kidding, right now I'm feeling giddy and its 6:20 PM on Friday evening!!

Thanks for Everything!

David – Senior Sales Consultant

Dave,

In regard to the training sessions, I have learned too many lessons to mention. Points that stick out in my mind in general are the need to follow the step of sale process as close to the letter as possible. Be constantly aware of the step you are in at all times. Confirm with the prospect on each call that they are also at the same step in the process including the timeframe for a decision. By doing this it will ensure that I will forecast the account more accurately.

After the initial training class I attended in Atlanta, I now constantly review with my prospects the negative and positive impact/outcome that is driving the business decision towards a solution. I am very aware of the need for a compelling need to not only purchase, but to move forward in the sales process. I now ask myself, "Have I given the prospect a compelling need to continue having dialog with me to purchase". I also ask the prospect, "What do you see as the compelling need to investigate our technology and/or invest in our solution?" It's all about compelling need! Have I given one? Do they have one?

Thank you again for a very applicable and practical training course.

Dave – Senior Sales Consultant

Dave,

I need to tell you about a recent call we made. You would have been proud of us at this account. While we were opening our discussions, rather than presenting our product I simply asked a 'thinking question' about the customer's goals and expectations. "What positive impact are you expecting by implementing a solution?" The customer opened up like a fountain giving us not only his expectations along with facts and figures, but also an outline of their strategies and initiatives.

Thanks for taking the time with us,

Jeff – Senior Sales Consultant

Dave,

Larry and I had a great day yesterday. We spent four hours in front of two customers. We received one commitment to buy and one commitment to proceed with a sample and a demo. Going into our second call, Larry and I agreed not to talk about our product or bring out a sample or brochure for a minimum of 15 minutes. Instead, we would just listen to the customer's concerns and qualify them. I believe we made it 25 minutes! In the end, it added tremendously to the quality of the call.

Thanks,

Scott – Senior Sales Consultant

Dave,

Thanks for lighting a fire under us about the subject of why deals slip. I had gone dark since our kickoff meeting in January in order to stay focused, primarily because my entire pipeline started to slip! However, since I see I am not alone in the 'Why Do They Slip' experience, I will now be working the methods you taught us because we all need effective solutions to address this problem.

Thanks,

Brian – Senior Sales Consultant

Hi Dave,

As usual, great exercise! Your 'Why Do They Slip?' book is very thought provoking. It challenges me to utilize approaches that I would not have considered and will ultimately cause me to step out of my regular approach and broaden my customer engagement skills.

Thanks for putting these coaching strategies together. I will definitely use this tool.

Rob – Senior Sales Consultant

Dave,

The information contained in the 'Why Do They Slip?' book is amazing! This should be called the Salesman's Bible! Study this information right before making every call!

Jay – Senior Sales Consultant

Dave,

I have been using the Value Letter after survey calls as a way of confirming my conversation with the prospect and more importantly as a framework for the survey call itself. Knowing that I am going to send the letter forces me to ask better questions to uncover the customer's compelling needs and business objectives.

Thanks,

Larry – Senior Sales Consultant

Dave,

FYI. As a result of the training, Rob's productivity has increased tremendously in Q1.

Emile – VP Sales, North America

Dave,

Rick, my top sales rep is an animal with this approach. It is my goal that everyone on my team will be using this technique regularly by the time you come to Chicago in April for our regional meeting

Thanks,

Chuck — Central Region Sales Director

Team,

Investing in professional sales communication and skillfully guiding each customer through the sales cycle works. On our team, Harry has developed a series of professional 'Value Letters' that he is using with good success.

Take the Leap!

Ralph — North East Regional Sales Director

Hi Dave,

I have closed three deals recently. In all three deals, I used the 'Value Letter' during the sales process and also included it in the executive summary sections of the proposals. I know it helped.

Thanks,

Rick — Senior Sales Consultant

Dave,

The type of discussion you highlighted in the recent competitive report takes place on almost every call. This was the best competitive information we have received yet in the 26 years I have been with the company.

Thanks,

Tom — Senior Sales Consultant

Dave,

I really learned a lot about the way we need to deliver our value proposition. Before this exercise, I knew how to talk about most of the value our product delivers to customers. However, I didn't have the glue to make them appear like one value statement.

Thanks,

Brian — Senior Sales Consultant

Dave,

I see the Value Proposition as an automatic door opener to help me engage perspective customers. I am printing 20 copies immediately and will reprint when necessary. This Value Proposition will win us business! By the way, the "Building the Value Bridge" graphic is great!

Thanks,

Rick — Senior Sales Consultant

Dave,

The Value Proposition can be used for every survey call. It creates an opportunity to talk about the customer's business needs and gets us focused on what is important to our prospect. In the process we can more effectively position our solution. If we show value, we advance the sale. It's that simple!

Thanks,

Carl – Senior Sales Consultant

Dave,

After your course in Atlanta I used the process with one of my working opportunities…Success! Then, I used the same approach with another account…Success again! Two deals closed!

Thanks for Your Help Dave,

Michael – Senior Sales Consultant

Dave,

I was very enlightened by your latest exercise. I now feel very confident in going up against the competition. The information is compelling and coupled with the Value Proposition, I am jazzed up and ready to attack!

Thanks,

Ed – Senior Sales Consultant

Dave,

I will have one of the value proposition handouts with me and available to use in every survey call. I know if I use it effectively I will be raising the discussion to the highest level of professionalism, which will only serve to enhance the perception of my company.

Thanks for doing this, Dave. When we are prepared, we are less likely to be caught off guard by the competition.

Brian – Senior Sales Consultant